Human Roots for Young Readers

Volume Two

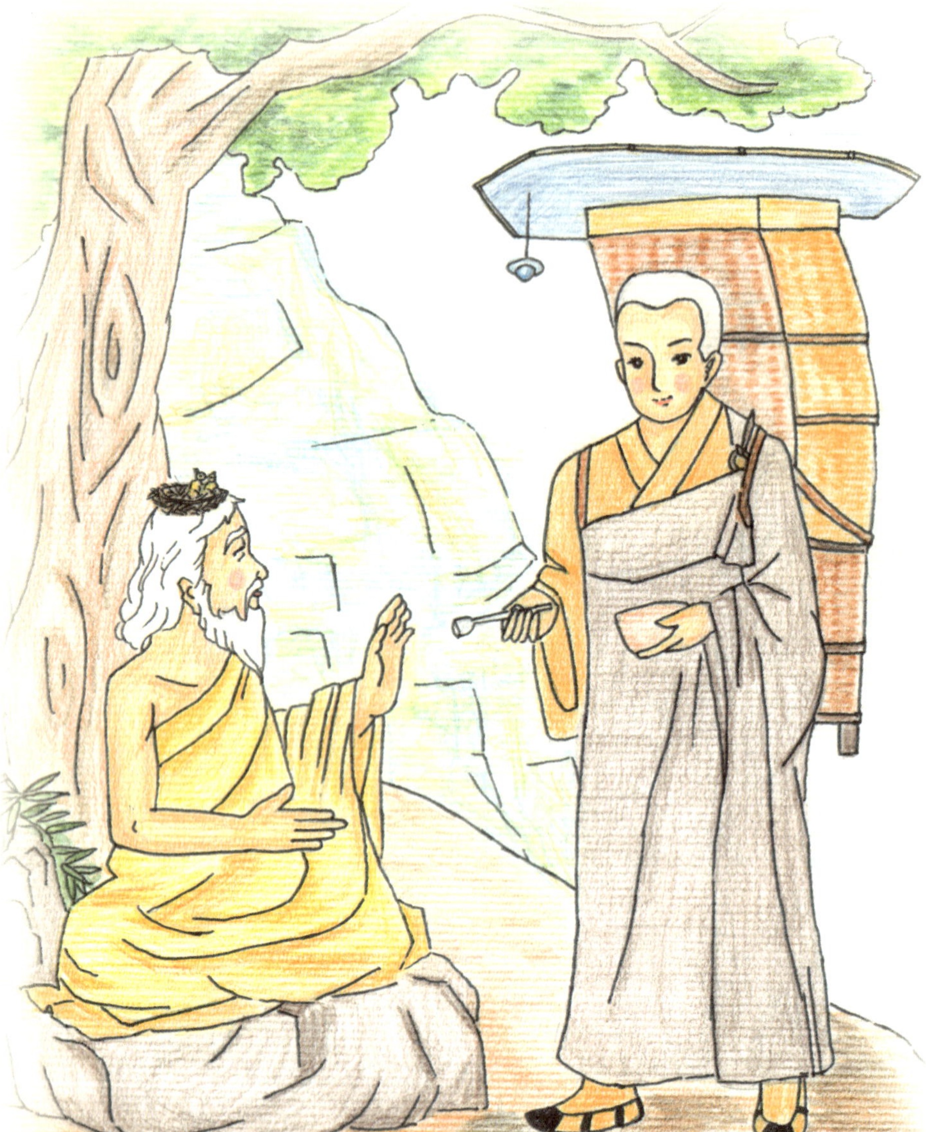

Human Roots
for
Young Readers
Volume Two

Translated and published by the
Buddhist Text Translation Society
Dharma Realm Buddhist University
Dharma Realm Buddhist Association
Burlingame, California U.S.A.

Human Roots for Young Readers

Published and edited by:
Buddhist Text Translation Society
1777 Murchison Drive, Burlingame, California 94010-4504

© 2001 Buddhist Text Translation Society
    Dharma Realm Buddhist University
    Dharma Realm Buddhist Association

Editing by Rebecca Lee
Illustrations by Fu Pi

First English edition 2001
Second Printing 2003

10 09 08 07 06 05 04 03   10 9 8 7 6 5 4 3 2

Printed in Taiwan, R.O.C.

    Addresses of the Dharma Realm Buddhist Association branches are listed at the back of this book.

          Library of Congress Cataloging-in-Publication Data

    Human roots for young readers / translated and published by the Buddhist Text Translation Society, Dharma Realm Buddhist University, Dharma Realm Buddhist Association.-1st ed.
    p.cm.
    Includes bibliographical references and index.
    Contents: v. 1. At the time of the Buddha : stories of the Buddha's disciples -
    Summary: A collection of traditional Buddhist stories, adapted for modern youth, including tales of Buddha, his disciples, and the Bodhisattvas.
    ISBN 0-88139-317-7 (v.1 pbk.) - ISBN 0-88139-318-5 (v.2 pbk.)
    1. Buddhist stories, English. (1. Buddhist stories. 1. Jataka stories.) I. Buddhist Text Translation Society. II. Dharma Realm Buddhist University. III. Dharma Realm Buddhist Association.

BQ1032 .H86 2002
294.3'8-dc21

                                                                                   2001043436

Table of Contents:

Part 3 Buddhism Goes to China and Other Stories

2	Introduction
3	A Treasure of India
5	A Child Lifts an Incense Burner
13	The Pine Needles Point to the East
20	The Three-Cart Patriarch
27	Reciting the Buddha's Name
30	The Lotus Flower
31	Ice-lotus Monk
33	The Old Monk's Horse
36	A Kind Monk Feeds the Birds

Part 4 Planting Good Seed

42	Introduction
44	Trapped
48	Saving Ants
52	The Poor Man and the Rich Man
54	A visit to King Yama
58	Thirty-two Women Repair a Buddha Image
61	The Thief and the Spider
64	Never Steal from your Parents
67	The Foolish Farmer of Sung
69	The Big Bear
73	Lion's Milk
79	The Snake and the Seven Pots of Gold
84	The Upside-down Dragon
87	How People Came to be on Earth

104	GLOSSARY

Part 3

*Buddhism Goes to China
and Other Stories*

Introduction

The two children raced through the meadow of wildflowers and plunked down under their favorite pine tree. The silence was broken only by bird calls and the wind's song. "What are you reading?" asked Lillian, gazing at the sky through a hazy green of shimmering pine needles.

"The *Shurangama Sutra*," said her brother, Ivan. "It's the most important teaching spoken by the Buddha. It teaches us to be generous and kind and wise."

"What is a Sutra?" asked Tiki, their little bird friend. It swooped down from a tree branch and landed on Ivan's shoulder.

"Sutras are the sacred writings of the Buddha," said Ivan. "Let me explain. Sutra means 'stringing together', like a necklace."

"Like this?" asked Lillian, holding up a garland of wildflowers that she was making.

Ivan said, "Yes. The Buddha never wrote anything himself. His disciples memorized his words and passed them down by word of mouth. It was not until several hundred years after the Buddha's death that his teachings were written down. Now the Sutras are in many languages, even English. How lucky we are!

"Long ago, the kings of India did not allow the Sutras to leave the country. However this did not keep Buddhism from going to China and to other countries. I have some great stories to tell…"

Tiki nestled against Ivan's collar ready for the stories to begin.

A Treasure of India

"You can't take this Sutra out of India. It's the Shurangama Sutra, a national treasure!" the guards shouted at Dharma Master Paramita at the border of India and China.

"I wish to go to China and take the Sutra with me. It's important for the people there to have it. May I please have permission to pass?"

"No one has permission, not even you!"

"If I'd been there, I would have carried it across the border for him, and no one would have known," cried Tiki.

"But since you weren't there, the Master turned back to India. But he didn't give up. He had a plan. Listen to the story," said Ivan.

He wrote the Sutra out in tiny letters on very fine silk. Then he rolled it up tightly and sealed it with wax. Taking a knife, he cut back the skin on his arm and placed the roll of Sutras underneath the skin. He patched up his arm and healed the wound with herbs.

Once again, he tried to cross the border into China. "Let the Master pass into China. He's not carrying anything," said a guard at the border, after searching him.

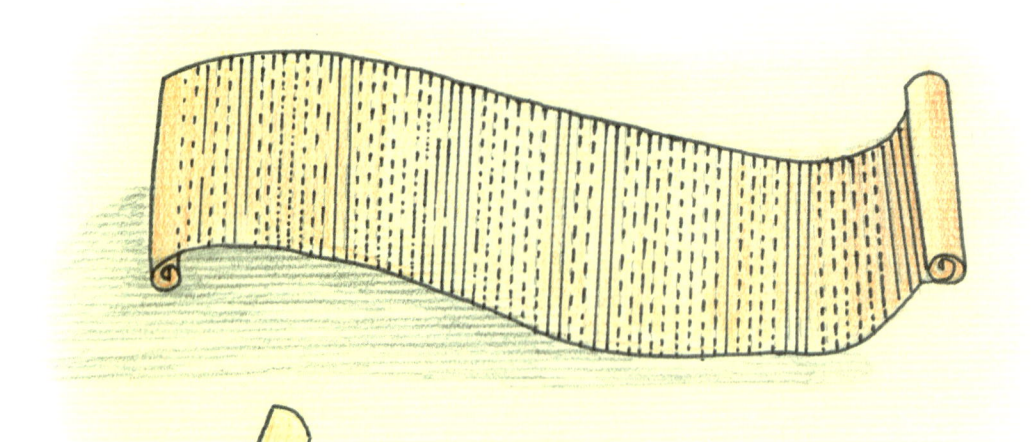

Dharma Master Paramita walked all the way from India to China. He climbed rugged mountains and passed through desert lands. The journey was dangerous and long, but he made it. Once in China, he went to Canton Province and lived in a temple where he translated the Shurangama Sutra into Chinese.

"When he finished, he went straight back to India. Do you know why?" asked Ivan.

"Let me guess. From what I know about this Dharma Master, he must have gone back to turn himself in. I don't think he could live a lie."

"That's just what he did. He went to the king and asked for his punishment," said Ivan.

A Child Lifts an Incense Burner

Kumarayana was the son of a Prime Minister. His father wanted him to follow in his footsteps, but he had other plans. He left home and became a monk. In his travels, he went to the country of Kucha near the border of India. There the king of Kucha invited him to the palace to speak the Dharma. The king had a beautiful young sister named Jiva. When she saw Kumarayana, she said to her brother, the king, "I want to marry this man."

By imperial command, Kumarayana was forced into giving up being a monk to marry Jiva.

After many years, Jiva was to have a child. While her son was in her womb, she grew in wisdom and learning. An Arhat said to her, "Your child will be great in wisdom. He will be a famous Dharma Master one day. His name will be Kumarajiva."

"Kumarajiva!" His mother's voice floated past the courtyard and up to the tree to where Kumarajiva was watching a nest of baby birds. He hurried to answer her call.

"Here I am, mother," he said, catching his breath. It was a warm summer day.

His mother stopped chopping vegetables and wiped her hands on her floral apron. She picked up a basket and tucked it under her arm, "We're going to the temple to make an offering of rice and vegetables to the monks and nuns," she said.

Kumarajiva was very happy to go with his mother. He followed her through the backyard where the cows lived. A little calf ran over to greet him. He bowed to his little friend and wished it a good day. "Namaste!" he said, with a clear smiling voice. Then he ran out the gate to catch up with his mother.

While his mother went to the temple kitchen, Kumarajiva stayed in the main hall. There were many beautiful things on the altar—golden images of the Buddha, lighted lamps, vases of flowers, and a huge incense holder called a censor.

"What a huge censor! I'll offer it to the Buddha," said Kumarajiva, and lifted it over his head. Then he thought, "I am just seven years old. How can I lift this heavy urn?"

As soon as he had the thought, he dropped the censor on the floor. Suddenly he knew. "Everything is made from the mind alone.

As soon as I thought about lifting the urn, I dropped it."

On the way home, he asked his mother, "May I leave home and become a monk?"

His mother was not surprised, but she was not sure if his father would agree. "I'll have to ask your father first," she said, making a plan.

The next day, Kumarajiva heard his mother say to his father, "I wish to become a nun."

"Before I married you, I was a monk myself. But now that we are married, I've grown fond of you and don't want to lose you," his father said.

"Then I won't eat or drink. I'll starve myself," said his mother. Kumarajiva knew she would get her way.

For six days, his mother did not eat or drink anything. Her husband cared for her very much and wanted the best for her. Finally he said, "I'm afraid you're going to starve to death. If leaving home means this much to you, then you have my permission, but please eat something first."

"Call in a Dharma Master to cut my hair," she said, "then I'll eat." After her hair was cut, she ate. Then she asked her husband, "Will you allow Kumarajiva to leave home with me?"

Kumarajiva's father smiled and said, "The answer is yes. I see that he's unusually wise for his age. Anyway, I don't want you to fast again."

So Kumarajiva and his mother left the home life, while his father continued his work as Prime Minister, helping the people and his country.

Kumarajiva was very happy as a monk and studied hard. Once he read a Sutra, he never forgot it. In one day, he could memorize more than thirty-six thousand words. Soon he could recite all the Sutras by heart. Over the years he became one of the most famous Dharma Masters in India.

In China it was predicted that a great sage would someday come to their country. When Emperor Fu Chin heard of Kumarajiva, he said to his general, Lu Guang, "Take 70,000 soldiers to India and escort Kumarajiva here to China. He is a sage."

It just so happened that Kumarajiva's dream was to take the Buddha Dharma to China. So he didn't mind being escorted there at all.

One night on the way back to China, Lu Guang made camp in a small valley. Kumarajiva told him, "This is not a safe place. There will be a storm here tonight and many will drown."

Lu Guang scoffed at him. "You're a monk. What do you know about military affairs?"

That night, a strong wind came up and blew fiercely. Rain fell heavily. By morning, most of the army and horses had been swept away and were lost in the storm.

Lu Guang said, "I wish I had listened to Kumarajiva. Now I know he's a very special person."

Once in China, Kumarajiva learned Chinese and began to translate the Sutras from Sanskrit into Chinese. Sanskrit is one of the languages that Sutras were written in at that time.

The emperor set up a translation center in the capital city of Chang An. There Kumarajiva translated over three hundred volumes of Sutras.

When it was time for Kumarajiva to leave the world, he said, "I don't know if my translations of the Sutras are correct or not. If they are correct, my tongue will not burn when I am cremated." When his body was cremated, the fire did not touch his tongue.

Everyone likes Kumarajiva's translations of the Sutras. People say that they are simple and easy to understand and are the same as the Buddha's heart. One of the most important Sutras he translated was the Amitabha Sutra.

Kumarajiva's name means 'youth of long life". One could say, "He is young in years, but has the wisdom of an old, old man."

The Pine Needles Point East

Long ago in the Tang Dynasty in China, there lived an official who was very poor. The other officials cheated people out of their hard-earned living, but the poor official never cheated anyone. He only helped people.

One day, the official took his youngest son to a Buddhist temple. There the boy heard the story about the Buddha giving up his life for a tigress. On the way home that night, he gazed at the immense, starry sky and wondered about the beauty of the Buddha's teachings. "I shall become a monk," he told his father, the official.

At the age of thirteen, the boy became a monk and went to live in a temple. Wherever the Buddha Dharma was being lectured, he would go. He was up and walking from the first glimpse of daylight until the blue shadows of dusk turned into night. The more he heard the Dharma, the more he was filled with the joy and wonder of life. Five years passed and he became ordained as Dharma Master Hsuan Tsang.

Hsuan means "wonderful" and Tsang means "awe-inspiring". This meant that he was very wise and could do what others could not do.

The Master said, "I have heard the Dharma spoken in many different ways, but what am I supposed to believe? I don't know what is true and what is false. I should go to India where the Buddha was born to learn the truth."

Full of hope, he went to see Emperor Tai Tsung and asked, "Son of Heaven, I wish to travel to India to bring the Buddha Dharma back to the Imperial Palace. May I have permission to travel on one of your trade ships?"

The emperor had heard Dharma Master Hsuan Tsang speak Dharma many times and was very fond of him. He was afraid that the Master would not return to China, so he promptly answered, "I forbid you to go to India on the imperial ships."

The Master bowed his head and replied, "I prefer that the Son of Heaven cut off my head if I cannot seek the truth." But the emperor could not be persuaded.

So the Master began to prepare for the trip to India on his own. "There are rugged mountains to climb and wide rivers to cross," he said to himself. "But how can I learn to climb mountains? There are none around here."

Suddenly he came up with a plan. He piled stools and tables on top of each other until they reached to the ceiling. "This is better than real mountains!" he cried, leaping from stool to table until he reached the top of the pile. Then he jumped down and climbed back to the top again and again.

"What kind of fool is this?" asked the other monks when they saw him.

Soon the Master was ready for the trip. He returned to the emperor and said, "I am leaving for India."

The emperor was puzzled. "How can you leave? I will not give you a ship or an army to guard you?"

"With the blessings of the Son of Heaven, I will travel alone over land."

"It will be a most dreadful journey. I fear for your life, but I can not stop you." the emperor said with dismay. "When will you be back?"

"See that pine tree. The needles are pointing to the west. When they are pointing to the east, I will return," the Master replied.

The next morning hundreds of people lined the streets with tears in their eyes and prayers in their hearts for the Master's safe return. The emperor reluctantly opened the west gate of the city to let his dear friend pass through. Dharma Master Hsuan Tsang was off to India.

For many years, the Master traveled through the treacherous mountains of the north and the wastelands of Siberia. He passed through a land where he saw not one living soul, a wild and desolate land where not even a blade of grass was to be seen. There was no water, no food, no shelter; only lizards scurrying under rocks and snakes slithering along cracked ground under the harsh sun. And he also passed through lands of abounding beauty and mystery.

On the way, the Master joined other travelers and shared meals with them. Other times, he traveled alone and went hungry. But no matter where he went, he marveled at the beauty and wonders of the universe. At last he reached the enchanted land of India.

The Master found life in India very difficult. Everything was strange to him—the people, the language. "You must first study Sanskrit," the great Dharma Masters told him. "Then you can understand what we have to teach."

So the Master set out to learn Sanskrit. Once he did, he traveled all over India and learned everything he could about the Dharma. He walked on the same roads as the Buddha and drank water from the same streams.

He visited the place where the Buddha gave up his life for the tigress and sat in meditation under the Bodhi tree.

The Master never looked down on any one in India, no matter

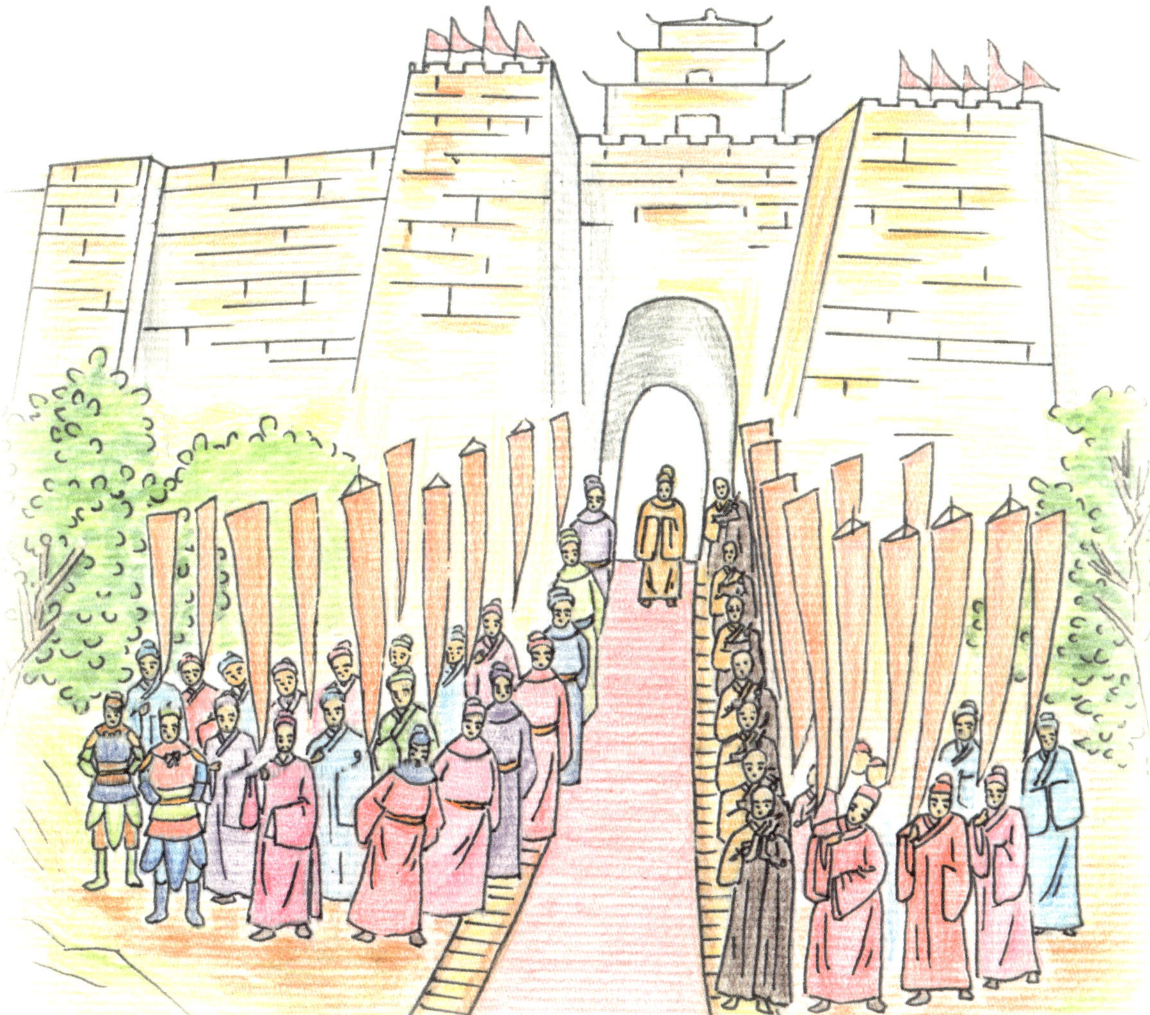

how little they knew. Like his father, he was a friend to everyone.

After nineteen years, his mission was completed. He appeared before the king of India and asked, "It is time for me to return to China. May I travel back on one of your trade ships?"

"I will not give you permission," said the king. He had grown fond of the Master and did not want him to leave India.

"Then I will have to travel back overland," said the master.

Early one morning, Emperor Tai Tsung was strolling in his garden. Some dewdrops, glistening on pine needles, caught his eye. The needles were pointing to the east. "It is time for Master Hsuan Tsang to return. Let us go to the west gate to welcome him back." When they opened the gate, the Master was waiting for them.

The Master explained the Sutras and all that he had learned in India to Emperor Tai Tsung. "How wonderful! How wonderful are the Buddha's teachings!" said the emperor, "They are more fragrant than a peach blossom, more beautiful than the song of the nightingale, and more precious than gold. May the people of China cherish and protect them forever."

Master Hsuan Tsang began to translate the Sutras from Sanskrit into Chinese. Eight hundred monks helped him. When the Great Prajna Sutra was translated, the peach trees blossomed six times, their sweet fragrance spreading the Dharma throughout the land of China.

The Three-Cart Patriarch

The Bird's Nest

On the trip to India, Master Hsuan Tsang had many adventures. Out of these adventures came a host of stories that are woven into the historical tapestry of Buddhism. The following story is the one most told.

As this story comes off the loom, it weaves its way high into the mountains where Master Hsuan Tsang was following the traces of an old footpath. It crossed over and over a gray river that roared and tumbled down over-hanging rocks into the valley below. The path led him to a cave where an old cultivator was sitting in meditation.

The old cultivator, who had been sitting for so long, seemed to be growing out of the earth. Layers of dust covered his ragged robes. Bugs and ants scurried across his spindly arms and a snake lay curled around his ankle. The soft peeping of birds could be heard from a nest nestled in his matted hair. Little beaks like scissors waited for supper.

"I must awaken him!" said the Master and rang the handbell. "R-a-ling! Ring-a-ling! Ring-a-ling!"

Slowly an eye cracked open and peered at the Master. Two lips parted and a handful of teeth danced to the ground. His voice crackled like a dried leaf. "Why did you ring the bell?"

"Old Cultivator, what's the sense in sitting so long in meditation?" the Master asked. Getting no answer, he leaned close and shouted once more into the old man's ear.

The other eye opened, "I'm waiting for the Red Buddha to come

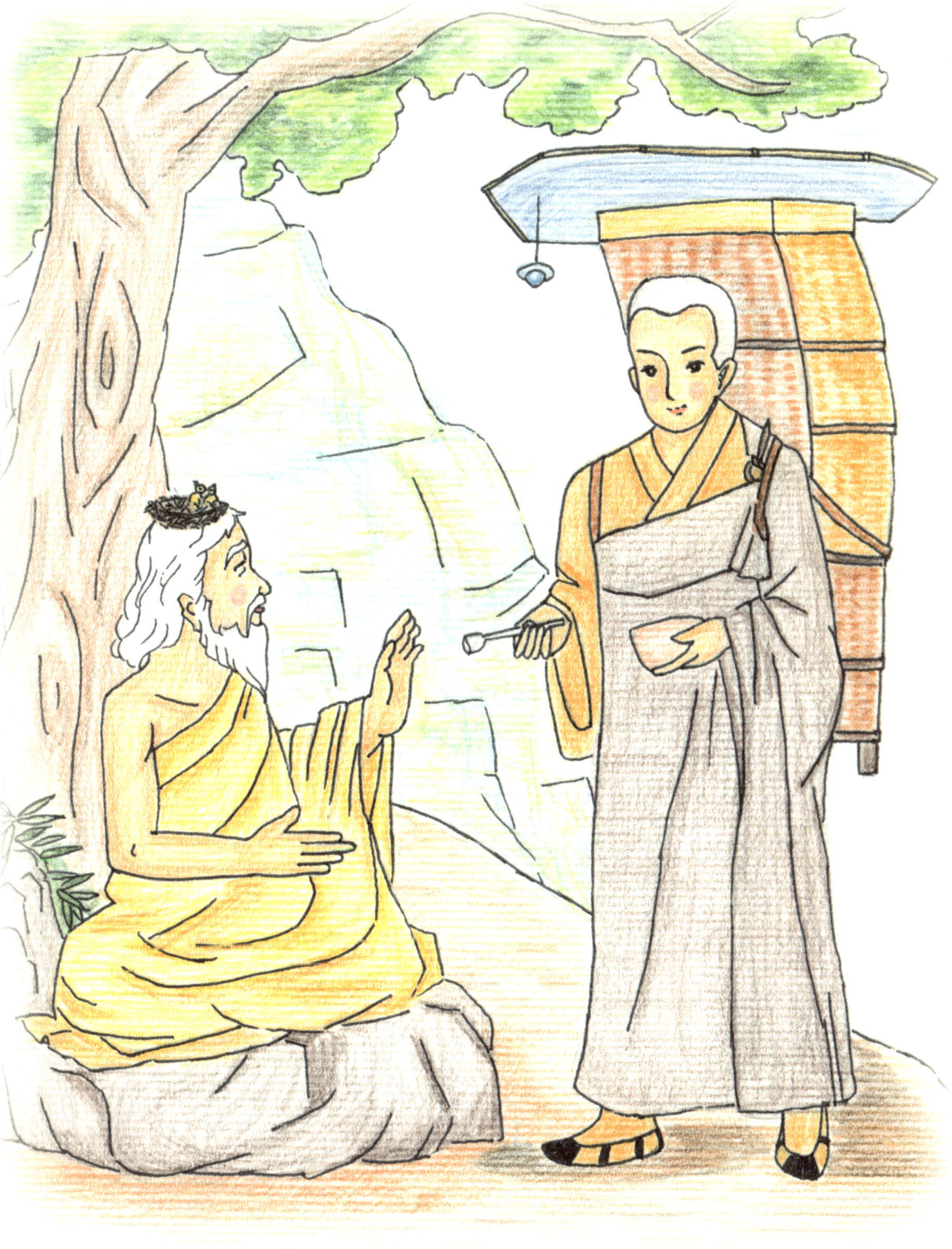

into the world. I'm going to help him teach the Buddha Dharma."

"But he has already come and gone. His name was Shakyamuni Buddha. You just sat there and missed him," said the Master.

"Well, what time is it?" squeaked the old cultivator.

"It's the Tang Dynasty."

"That's all right," the old cultivator's eyes closed. "If the Red Buddha has come and gone, I will wait for the White Buddha."

"Don't go back into meditation!" said the Master. "The Buddha's teachings are still in the world. Now is the time to teach the Buddha Dharma. Come along with me and help!"

"Very well, I'll go," said the old cultivator, but when he moved his legs to get up, they crumbled into dust.

The Master sighed, "Your body is too old. You'll have to leave it and be reborn into a new one. Listen carefully. Go to the yellow-tiled house in Chang An in China and be reborn there. I'll look for you when I return from India."

So the old cultivator went off to rebirth in China and Master Hsaun Tsang went on his way to India to bring back the Sutras.

When the Master returned to China, he visited the emperor and said, "I came to see your new son."

"But there has been no prince born here," the emperor said.

"No?" said the Master, puzzled, "Then I will have to look into this."

He soon found out that the old cultivator had gotten it wrong. He had been reborn in the house with the blue tiles.

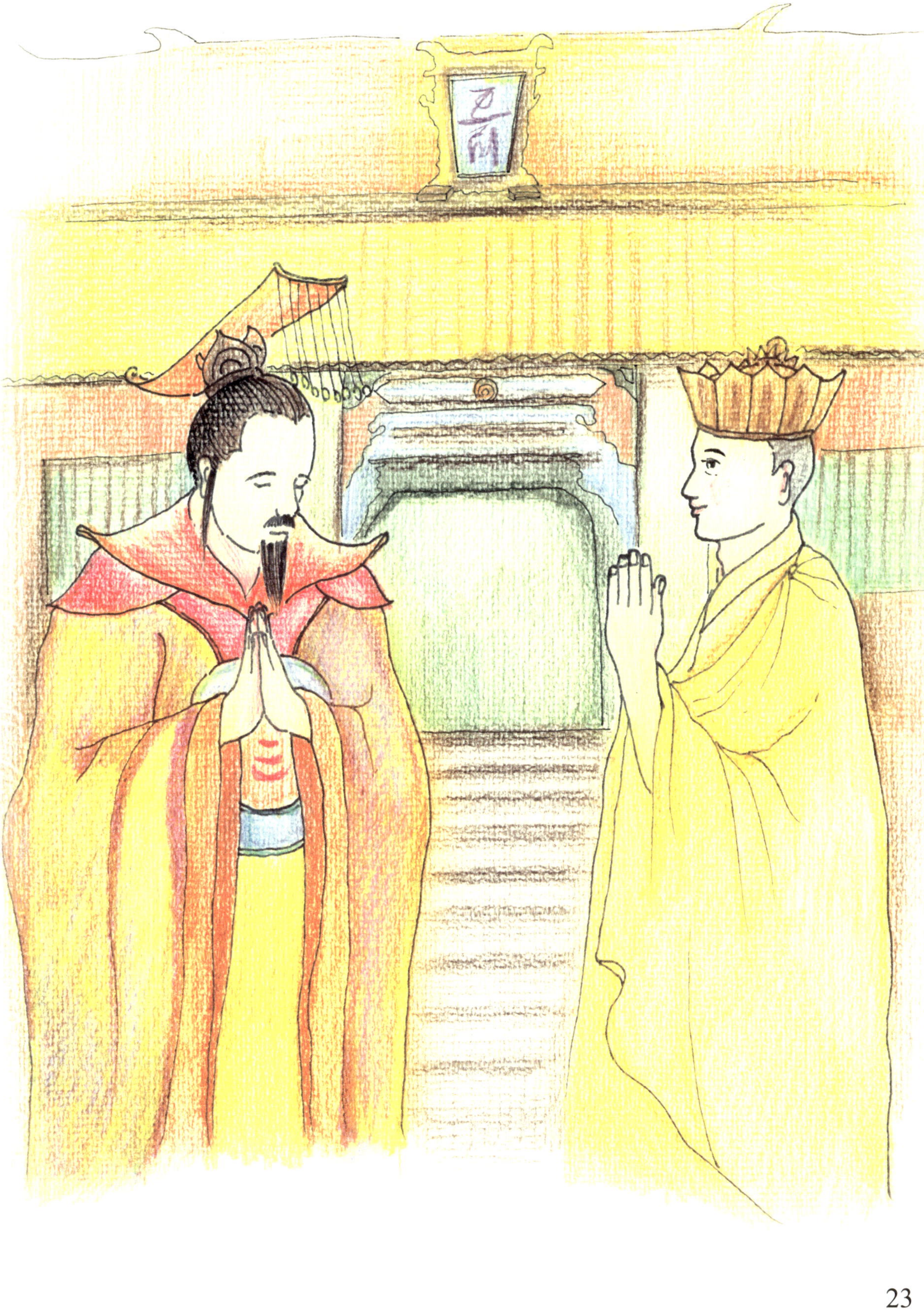

The House with Blue Tiles

Yu Chi Gung lived in the house with the blue tiles. He was the emperor's most flamboyant minister. He was a big man and a fearless warrior who protected the country. When he was not in battle, he liked to eat meat, drink wine, and entertain women.

A nephew was born in Gung's house with the blue tiles. He followed in his uncle's footsteps and did nothing but eat meat, drink wine, and entertain beautiful women. The Master was sure that the nephew was none other than the old cultivator himself, who had forgotten his promise.

Going to the house of Gung, the Master explained the mistake. Gung said, "Well, you told him to come, so you tell him to go!"

"I won't go!" snapped the nephew, when he was consulted.

So the Master went to the emperor and pleaded. "I need Gung's nephew to help me translate the Sutras. Give him whatever he wants."

The emperor said to the nephew, "You must leave home. This is an Imperial Order!"

"I'll leave home then," the nephew said. "But I want to take three things with me—a cart of meat, a cart of wine, and a cart of beautiful women." The emperor was shocked, but agreed.

The Ring of a Bell

Drums rolled! Dancers twirled! Acrobats tumbled! The streets were filled with festivity. Everyone had come to see Gung's nephew off to the monastery. Three carts followed him—one cart filled with meat, one cart filled with wine, and one cart filled with beautiful women.

25

The gate of Great Flourishing Monastery opened. A bell rang. When the nephew heard the bell, his eyes brightened and he said, "So that's the way it is. I was the old cultivator in the mountains. Tell Master Hsuan Tsang that Kuei Ji is here to help him translate the Sutras."

With a flick of his hand, he waved the carts away, "Take them back. I don't need them anymore."

The nephew was ordained as Dharma Master Kuei Ji. Since then he has been known as the 'Three-Cart Patriarch'. Of all the translators who helped Dharma Master Tsang, he was the foremost.

Reciting the Buddha's Name

Amitabha Buddha is the Buddha of Limitless Light and Limitless Life. He cast one long sweeping look into the hearts of all living beings on planet earth and said, "I will create a Buddha Land called the 'Land of Ultimate Bliss'." Anyone who recites my name or hears it will be reborn in this land upon his or her death. Those who are reborn there will be trained as Bodhisattvas so they can return to the world and help all those in need."

Once there was a monk who gathered fire wood for the temple and recited Amitabha Buddha's name. This poem is written in honor of him.

I'm Going for Sure

>Once there was a monk named Ching Hung
>Who gathered firewood for the temple.
>He recited Amitabha's name non-stop.
>His practice and life were quite simple.
>
>One winter day, said he, "I want to leave"
>The Abbot asked, "Can you wait?
>The meditation session is not over,
>Your leaving now puts us in a bad state."
>
>After the winter session was over,
>He asked, "May I leave now?"
>"But New Year's about to begin.
>In the cold, we can't manage somehow."
>
>He waited until the end of New Year.
>Then he said, "I'm going for sure!"
>The Abbot said, "That's just fine."
>He knew Ching Hung was sincere.

"I've lived with the monks for a long time,
May I ask them to please send me off?"
When the monks heard about the request,
Jealousy caused them to fume and to scoff!

"He's just an old monk who gathers wood.
Why does he get attention like this?"
The Abbot kindly answered,
"Bring the bell and the red wooden fish."

Into Ching Hung's room they gathered
Still scoffing til suddenly they saw
That he was going off to rebirth.
This left them in silence and awe.

Being wise, Ching Hung saw into his future.
It was time to go off to the Pure Land.
He sat up in full lotus and left,
His recitation beads held fast in his hand.

The monks recited Amitabha Buddha
From morning on through the night,
In honor of Ching Hung the monk
Who kept the fires of Buddhism burning bright.

The Lotus Flower

With its large leaves and bright blossoms, the lotus is the most beautiful of all the water lilies.

It is known as the "sacred flower" both in India and Egypt. In Buddhism, it is a symbol of Enlightenment.

> It grows out of mud through deep water,
> And opens into a beautiful flower above.
> Although it grows out of mud,
> It is not tainted, but perfectly pure.

The Buddha spoke the Dharma Flower Sutra during the last six years of his life. This Sutra teaches us how to develop our wisdom and to be content.

To study, memorize, or even hear it brings blessings and benefits that last for quadrillions of eons. Following are some accounts of these wonders.

The Ice-lotus Monk

There was once a monk who recited the Dharma Flower Sutra everyday. The Sutra is so long that it takes almost a whole day to recite it. One cold winter in Manchuria, a monk wrote out the entire Sutra word by word. When he dipped his brush into the water to rinse it out, the water froze and formed into a lotus flower on the brush tip. The lotus grew as large as a fruit bowl and emitted light. Because of what happened that day, the monk gave himself the name "Ice Lotus Monk". This story has been told and retold by those who saw it and believed it.

The Ice-lotus Monk

In wintry Manchuria's snow-covered ground,
Sheets of ice glimmer on the lakes all around.

Flocks of geese fly to the south in a flurry,
Past pale frosted panes in a lone monastery.

Stroke by stroke, creating each word,
A lone monk writes out a Sutra that he heard.

The universe flows through his hand with its power,
Commanding the birth of the sweet Dharma Flower.

Cleansing his brush in the cold, icy room,
The water-filled tip freezes into a lotus bloom.

The lotus grows larger; the room glows with light.
The Ice-lotus Monk is enlightened on this night.

Now all of the faithful, who seek and pray
Know writing out Sutras is a True Sage's Way.

The Old Monk's Horse

In the early days of China, an old monk rode an old gray horse to the palace where he served as advisor to the emperor. Along the way, he recited the Dharma Flower Sutra by heart. By the time he arrived at the palace, he had recited the first roll. At that time in China, books were written on paper and rolled up into long rolls.

One day, the old horse died suddenly. Nine months later, a son was born to a man and his wife. They lived near the temple and were devoted followers of the Buddha.

The parents were happy to have such a special son. Everyday they took him to the monastery to make offerings to the monks. The years went by and he grew up to be a fine boy.

One day the parents visited the temple, but when they were ready to go home, they could not find their son anywhere.

"He's with the old advisor," a young monk said.

Going to the hut of the old advisor, the parents found him. "This is my teacher," he said. "I want to stay with him and become a monk."

This was just what the parents were hoping for. "How fortunate to have our first born son become a monk!" they said. "Surely our blessings will increase."

But it so happened that the boy turned out to not be very smart at all. He couldn't learn to read and he couldn't learn to write. Try as they might, the monks could not teach him anything.

One day the old advisor was reciting the Dharma Flower Sutra inside the temple. The boy was walking by and heard him. He asked the advisor, "Will you please teach me this Sutra. I wish to memorize it."

To everyone's amazement, the boy memorized the first roll in no time at all. However, try as he might, he could not memorize the second roll.

"Why is this?" asked the old advisor and looked into the past. "Oh, now I understand. When I rode the old gray horse to court, I only recited the first roll. That is why the boy remembers it so well."

When he told the other monks about the boy, they said, "Just to think that from hearing the Dharma Flower Sutra, the horse was reborn as a person. There is that much merit and virtue from memorizing Sutras."

A Kind Monk Feeds the Birds

The Buddha taught people to recite mantras to calm their hearts and to bring about peace and happiness. A mantra is a group of harmonious sounds. The most important mantra that the Buddha taught is the Shurangama Mantra. This is a story about a kind monk who recited the Shurangama Mantra to birds.

Long ago in China, where the Yantze River flows, there lived a kind monk who explained the Shurangama Sutra so beautifully that the gods came down from the heavens to hear him. But people never came to listen. So the old monk decided to do something about it.

He bought a sack of birdseed and carried it on his back to the top of a twin-peaked mountain. And there on the twin-peaked mountain, he made his home in a cave.

Everyday as the sun rose above the mountains, he could be heard reciting the Shurangama Mantra over the seed. He would toss it into the wind and say, "Come, birds! Come eat!"

And the birds would flash and flutter through the blue morning sky, swirling, soaring, and swooping down to the ground. They would eat their fill, then fly away in a blur of color—red, blue, yellow, black, and brown.

Soon winter arrived on the twin-peaked mountain. The wind that blew from the north was cold. "Honk-honk-honk." The wild geese were flying south. But the sparrows and blue birds and other winter birds paid no attention to them. There was plenty of food on the mountain for them.

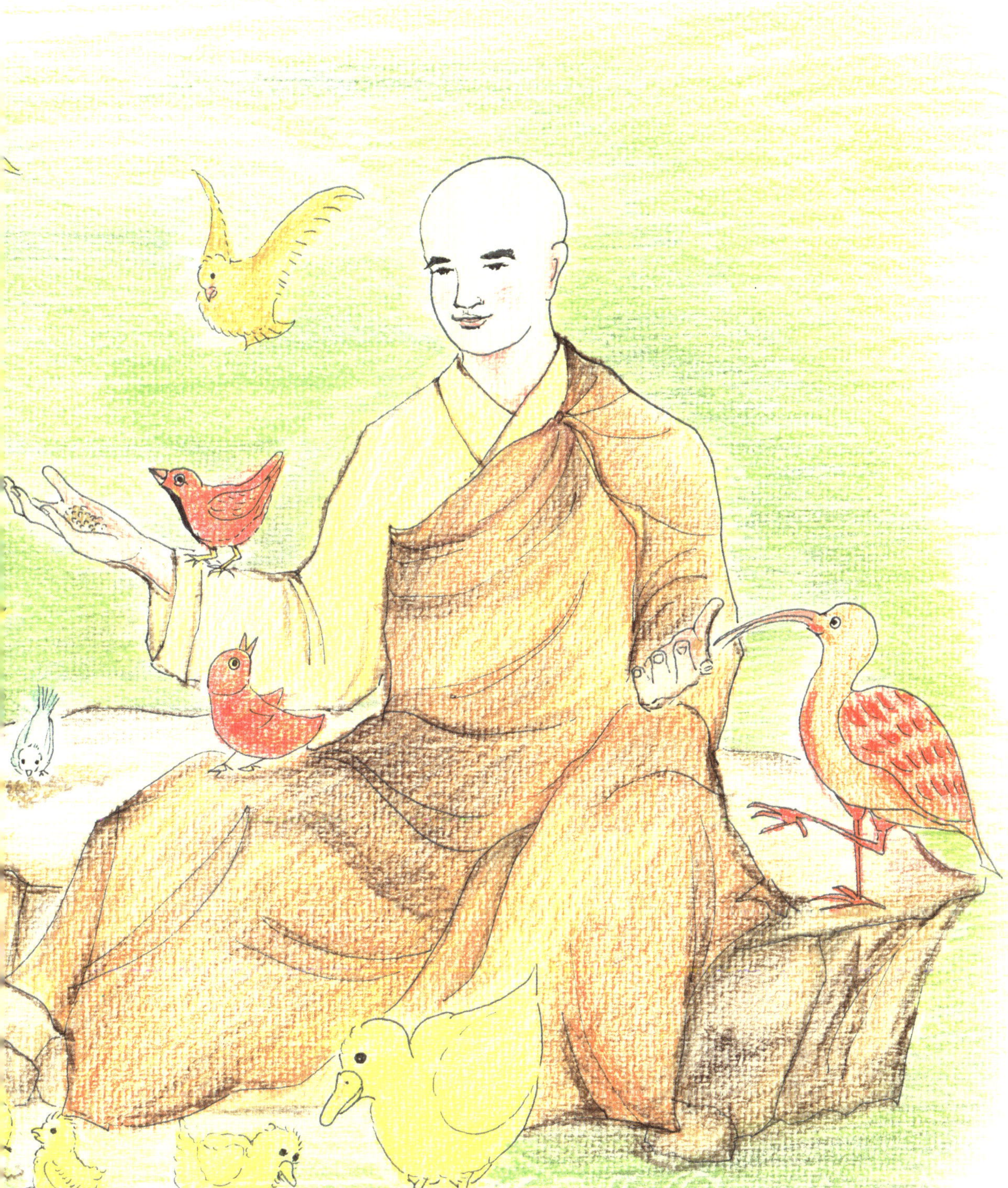

The grasses in the meadows were heavy with seeds.
And the pinecones were full of pine nuts.

But one night a big snowstorm came. Millions of snowflakes fell upon the mountain. By morning everything was covered with a blanket of snow. The winter birds came out from their hiding places and shook out their feathers. They looked in vain for food. They looked for the grass seed in the meadows. They flew from tree to tree and looked for pine nuts. But snow and ice covered everything. The birds were hungry.

As the sun rose above the mountain, clear and bright, the sharp eyes of the little birds saw an old monk coming toward them. He carried a bag of birdseed. "Come birds! Come eat!" He said, scattering the seeds on top of the snow, right and left. And as he scattered the seed, he recited the Shurangama Mantra. "Na mo he la da…"

"Food! Food!" called the birds. And all the birds who lived on the mountain in the winter heard the happy call. Soon the blue morning sky was filled with birds swirling and soaring and swooping to the ground. They ate their fill, then flew away in a blur of color—red, blue, yellow, black, and brown.

The snow melted. Spring came. Yellow and white flowers bloomed. The swallows came back from the south to build new nests. Soon there would be many mouths to feed. And there in the green meadows, the old monk could be seen planting millet and buckwheat and sunflowers and all the things that birds like.

Summer came next. Bird eggs hatched and wild cherries turned red. The grain in the meadows grew and grew.

Autumn followed summer and sweet persimmons dropped to the ground. "Thunk!" The old monk gathered the grains that he had planted and stored them for winter-feeding. For twenty years, the monk did this. Days and nights, summers and winters came and passed.

Then he returned to the city where the Yantze River flows. He explained the Sutras as beautifully as he had before. Again, the gods came down from the heavens to listen and this time people also came. They were happy, young people. To the surprise of everyone, when he began to teach the Shurangama Mantra, the young people already knew it. The old monk remembered the birds on the twin-peaked mountain and smiled.

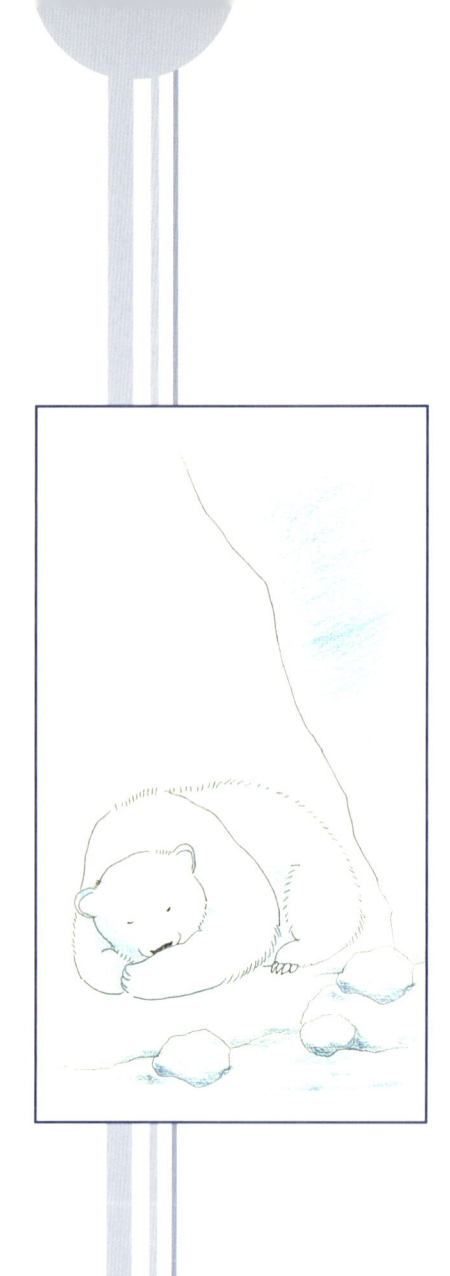

Part 4

Planting Good Seed

Introduction

Early one morning Ivan heard a loud "thump, thump" on the window. It was their friend Tiki, the little golden-winged bird. She frantically beat her wings on the window and screeched. "Help, help! Hunting season opened today and birds are being killed everywhere!"

Ivan's little sister Lillian ran into the room, "Tell the birds to come here. Our father doesn't allow hunting on our land."

"Why do people kill birds anyway? Just because they're people doesn't give them the right to kill us birds! It just isn't fair!" Tiki squawked, ruffling her feathers.

"They won't get away with it. You'll see!" said Lillian.

Ivan said, "There's a verse that the Buddha spoke.
> The kind of seed that is sown
> will produce that kind of fruit.
> Those who do good, will reap good results.
> Those who do evil, will reap evil results.
> If you carefully plant a good seed,
> Then you will joyfully gather good fruit.

It is the law of cause and effect in action and is called karma. It makes sense. We can see it everyday in our lives."

Tiki thought for a while, then asked, "Then it doesn't look too good for the hunters, does it?"

"Unless they change and stop killing birds and animals," said Ivan, "Karma is never off. I'll tell some stories to help explain more about it."

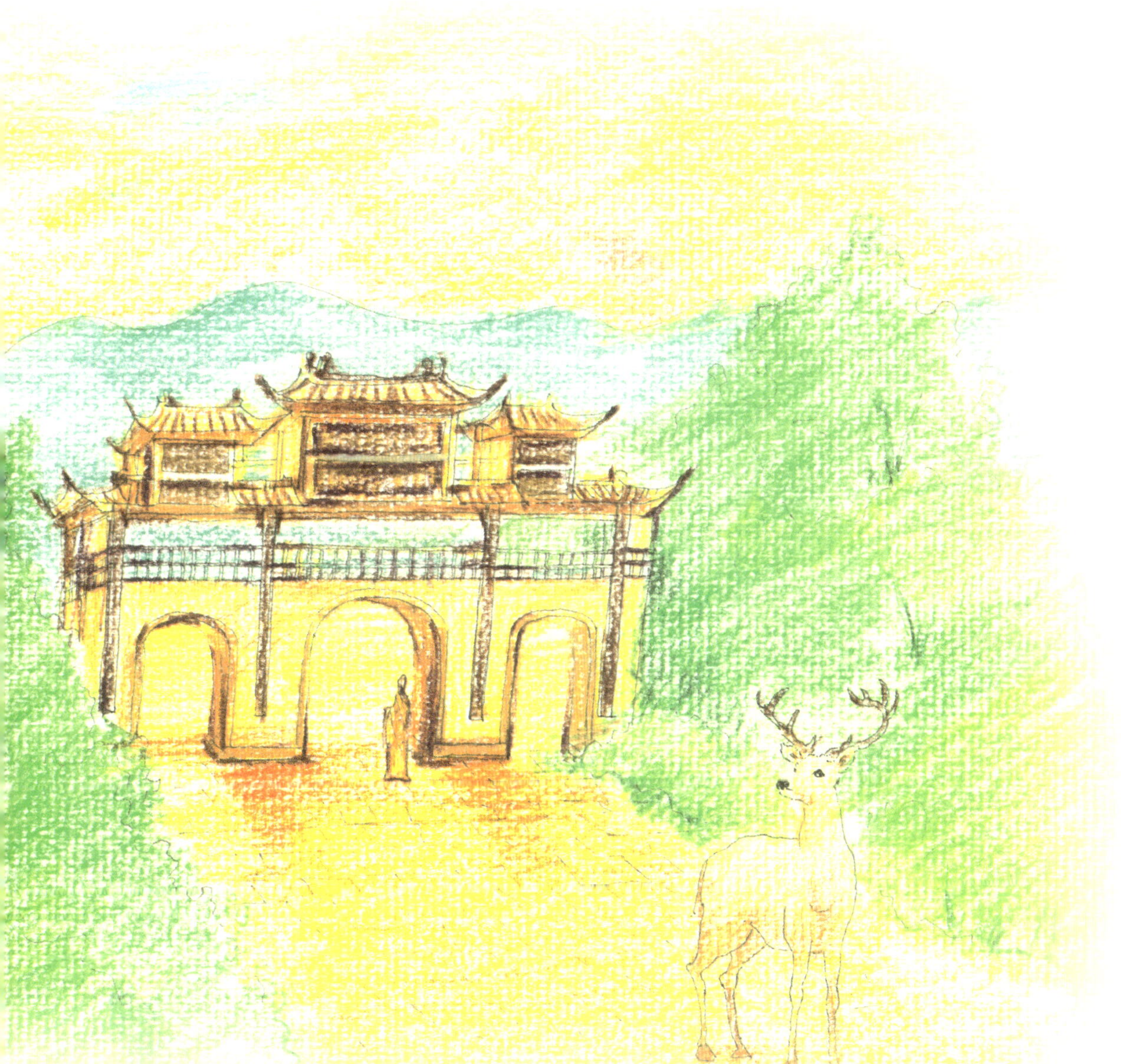

Trapped!

It was the middle of winter. The hunter looked out his window and said, "Bear tracks in the snow! So the big black bear is out prowling for food. Now is my chance to get him!"

Slinging a trap over his shoulders, he followed the bear's tracks into the woods. Soon he came to the den where the bear slept in the winter. Digging a deep hole in the earth, he set the trap into it. Carefully, he covered the top with branches and grass so the bear could not tell that it was a trap. Then he swept away his own tracks.

Rubbing his hands together, he said, "Now I must get far enough away so the bear can't smell me."

The hunter set off with his bow and arrow, whistling as he went, for he was sure to trap the bear. He was so busy thinking about his catch that he didn't notice where he was going.

Suddenly he realized that he was lost. His heart filled with fear. He had never been in this part of the woods before. Please let me find my way out, he begged silently, as he frantically picked his way through the thick forest. Looking up at the sky, enviously he watched a flock of birds flying beyond the circle of trees.

All of a sudden, he stumbled on some branches and fell down, down into a deep hole. He felt a stab of pain in his right leg. Something hard and sharp had clamped around it.

He pulled and pulled, but he couldn't get free. Every time he pulled, the trap bit deeper into his leg. "Help! I'm trapped!" he cried out in despair. But so far away in the woods, there was no one to hear him.

Before long, a blanket of darkness covered the hole. Night came, bringing with it cold and dampness. Huddling in a corner, the hunter groaned, "It's not fair. This trap was meant for a bear, not me. What a fool I am, I've set my own trap!"

In the deepest part of the night, the pain became unbearable. All he could think about was the bear roaming freely. If only I could trade places with the bear, he thought. Yet in his heart, he somehow knew that he was in the right place.

Morning came. The warmth of the new day streamed down into the hole and awakened the hunter. He heard the sound of crushing leaves on the ground above him. "Help!" he cried.

"Where are you?" a voice called back.

The hunter cupped his hands around his mouth and called out louder, "Down here in a bear trap."

The hand of a woodcutter reached down into the trap. Grabbing it, the hunter pulled himself out. "Thanks, Friend," he said.

The woodcutter took the hunter to his home and took care of him. When the hunter was well, he took up the work of wood-cutting. Often he walked by the place where he had set the trap, but never again did he trap or hunt another animal. Instead he helped the wild creatures that shared the forest with him.

Saving Ants

In a land far, far away, there once lived a poor man and woman who had a small son. The rain had not come to their village in a long time. The river was dry and the earth was cracked.

The young boy toiled beside his parents, working the hard crusty soil. But no matter how hard they worked, there was never enough food to eat. By and by, the boy grew weak and frail. His parents feared for his life.

Early one morning, as bats flew home on silent wings, the mother bundled up the child. Clutching him to her breast, she followed the river path that climbed steeply towards the eastern sky. The path led her to a gate. With her old bony hand, she clanged the bell.

Slowly the gate opened and a kind-looking old monk appeared. The woman and monk exchanged no more than a few words. She handed the sleeping child to the ancient one. Then she headed back home along the river.

Under the care of the old monk, the child soon became well and strong. He worked very hard sweeping the floors and tending the garden. When he was eight years old, he became a novice monk called a Shramana.

One day the little Shramana walked by the hut of a Dharma Master and heard him reciting a Sutra. He leaned against the door listening in silence. I hope the Master doesn't see me, he thought, or I'll be in big trouble.

"Open the door! Come on in!" a cheerful voice rang out.

The little Shramana jumped, "Who me?"

"Of course, of course. I've been expecting you."

"I-I couldn't help but listen," the little Shramana stammered. He quickly bowed to the Master.

All around the room were shelves filled with Buddhist books written on bamboo slits and bound with beautiful silk covers. Incense was burning from a censor. The Master motioned for the little Shramana to sit. "Today I will teach you the most important teaching of the Buddha. That is to be kind to everyone, even the small creatures that crawl upon the earth."

From then on, the little Shramana visited the Master everyday and listened to him tell stories of the Buddha's kindness. Often they would walk through the meadows or along the streams in the forests. When they came upon animals in trouble, they always helped them.

One day the Master looked into the future of the little Shramana and saw that he had only seven days to live. "I should send him home to his parents. It is not right for him to die in the forest," he told the monks.

Not wanting the boy to know his fate, the Master told him, "You may go visit your parents, but you must return in ten days." The little Shramana was very happy to visit his parents. Before the sun was up the next morning, he hurried down the rocky path. Wild roses were in yellow bloom and monkeys chattered in the trees.

Before long it began to rain. The wind blew and howled and there was lightning and thunder. By the side of the road, the boy spotted an ant hill. Water was gushing down the mountainside, heading straight for it. Ants were wildly scurrying about, back and forth, back and forth. If I don't do something quick, the ants will drown, the boy thought.

Using his bare hands, he dug a canal around the ant hill, to carry the water away. He dug and dug. But the water kept coming. "Faster! Faster!" he told himself and kept digging. And the water swirled and swirled and filled up the canal. Then it rushed down the side of the mountain. The ants were safe.

The rain stopped and the bright sun came out. The Little Shramana went on his way.

The poor man and woman were happy to see their son. "The river is alive again with flowing water and the earth is soft and fertile. There is enough food for everyone. You may stay and live with us now," they said.

"I promised that I would return to the monastery in ten days. I must keep my word, but I'll come back and visit you again soon," he said.

Ten days passed and the little Shramana was still alive. He said good-bye to his father and mother and returned to the mountain. When the Master saw him walking up the path, he was surprised. "Is this the boy still alive or is he a ghost?" Looking into the past, he saw how the little Shramana had rescued the ants.

"The boy was supposed to die in seven days," he told the other monks, "but because he saved the lives of the ants, he is still alive and will live for a very long time.

The Poor Man and the Rich Man

Early in the morning, a poor man packed his cart with the rice that he grew all year long. With his small cart loaded, he waved good-bye to his wife and pulled it down the road and over the hills to the market.

He sold the little rice that he had grown. And he bought some cloth and a needle for his wife. For himself, he bought a knife and he bought some salt. Then with his last coin, he bought a small pot of oil to light the lamps at the temple.

To the poor man's surprise, the Abbot met him at the main gate. He said, "Good man, have lunch with me." And the farmer lunched with the Abbot and went on his way.

It just so happened that a rich man came walking by. He said, "That poor man only gave a small pot of oil. And see how well he is being treated. If I offer 300 barrels of oil, the Abbot will surely treat me like a king."

So the next day, the rich man loaded his carts with 300 barrels of oil. With his carts loaded, he had them pulled down the road and over the hills to the temple.

The Abbot saw him and said to the gatekeeper, "Let the rich man in through the side door." He did not even go to meet him.

The other monks asked, "Why did you let that poor old man in through the main gate? He only gave a small pot of oil. The rich man gave 300 barrels of oil. Yet you let him in through the side door."

"The poor man used his last coin to buy the oil," the Abbot said. "The rich man could have easily given 3000 barrels of oil. What do you think? Who has the greater faith?"

A Visit to King Yama

Once there was a man who ate meat all his life. When he died, he came before King Yama. He was surprised to see King Yama talking to some pigs, chickens, sheep and other animals that had gathered around him.

King Yama asked the animals, "Do any of you know this man?"

A pig with the curliest tail said, "Oink! He ate a slice of bacon from my body!"

A fleecy white sheep said, "Baa! That's nothing! He ate a lamb chop from my baby lamb."

A speckled hen ruffled her feathers and said, "Cluck, cluck! I'm here to tell you that he ate all of me! Now it's my turn to eat him."

The man nervously started to make excuses. "It's not really my fault. If the meat hadn't been in the store, I wouldn't have bought it."

In a twinkling, the woman who owned the store was standing beside him. King Yama said to her, "Do you know that selling meat is not right? What do you have to say for yourself?"

The storekeeper looked at the sad eyes of a cow next to her and said, "I sell meat, but only because people want to buy it. If they didn't buy it, I wouldn't sell it."

55

The man who ate the meat said to her, "If you hadn't sold me the meat, I wouldn't have eaten it!"

"Look, it's not my fault and it's not your fault. The one who killed the animals is to blame. He's the one who should be here, not us," said the woman.

In another twinkling, the butcher was standing before the shop-keeper. He was wearing a bloody apron.

King Yama asked him, "Don't you know that killing animals is not right? What do you have to say for yourself?"

Tears filled the eyes of the animals as the butcher made excuses just as the other two had done. "I only kill the pigs and chickens because people want to eat them. How can it be my fault?"

"King Yama said to the man who ate meat, "There's no getting around it. If you ate pork, you must be reborn as a pig. If you are killed and eaten, then you have paid your debt to the pig. As for the other animals you have eaten, you must repay them, also."

"Wait a minute," pleaded the man. "It will take me many life-times to pay them all back before I can be reborn as a human again!"

King Yama silently looked at the man. Then he answered, "You should have thought of that before you took your first bite of meat."

At that, the butcher took off his bloody apron. The shop-keeper emptied her purse of coins. The butcher vowed to stop butchering animals. They decided to never eat meat again for they knew that one day they, too, would die and stand before King Yama.

NOTE: In many eastern religions, after death, souls goes before King Yama to be questioned about their deeds while on earth.

57

Thirty-three Women Repair a Buddha Image

Once, a long time ago, there was a poor woman named Shakra. One day when she was out picking berries, she came upon a ruined temple. The roof had fallen in and only the walls were standing.

Looking inside, she saw an image of the Buddha among the rubble. All the gold had worn off and the stone was a dull grey color.

Suddenly she noticed a dim light around the image. As she knelt in front of the image, the light grew brighter and brighter. A feeling of peace spread over her. "There's no roof to protect this Buddha, yet it still shines with light," she said aloud. "If only I had the money, I would rebuild this temple and replace the gold on the Buddha. But I am so poor, what can I do?"

A little mouse scurried out from behind the image and looked up at her. She smiled and said, "Ah, little one, you work hard all day looking for food and never give up. Then I will work as hard as you and find a way to repair the temple!"

She set out to find help. But the people in her village were as poor as she. At last she found thirty-two women to join her. Together they gathered firewood and berries and sold them, saving every coin they earned.

Soon there was enough money to begin the repairs. Slowly the temple was rebuilt and the Buddha image was gilded with gold. Now it shone brighter than ever.

As a result of their work repairing the temple, thirty two of the women were born in the Heaven of Thirty-three and each became a ruler of one heaven. Shakra was reborn as Lord Shakra and became ruler of the central heaven in the Heaven of Thirty-three.

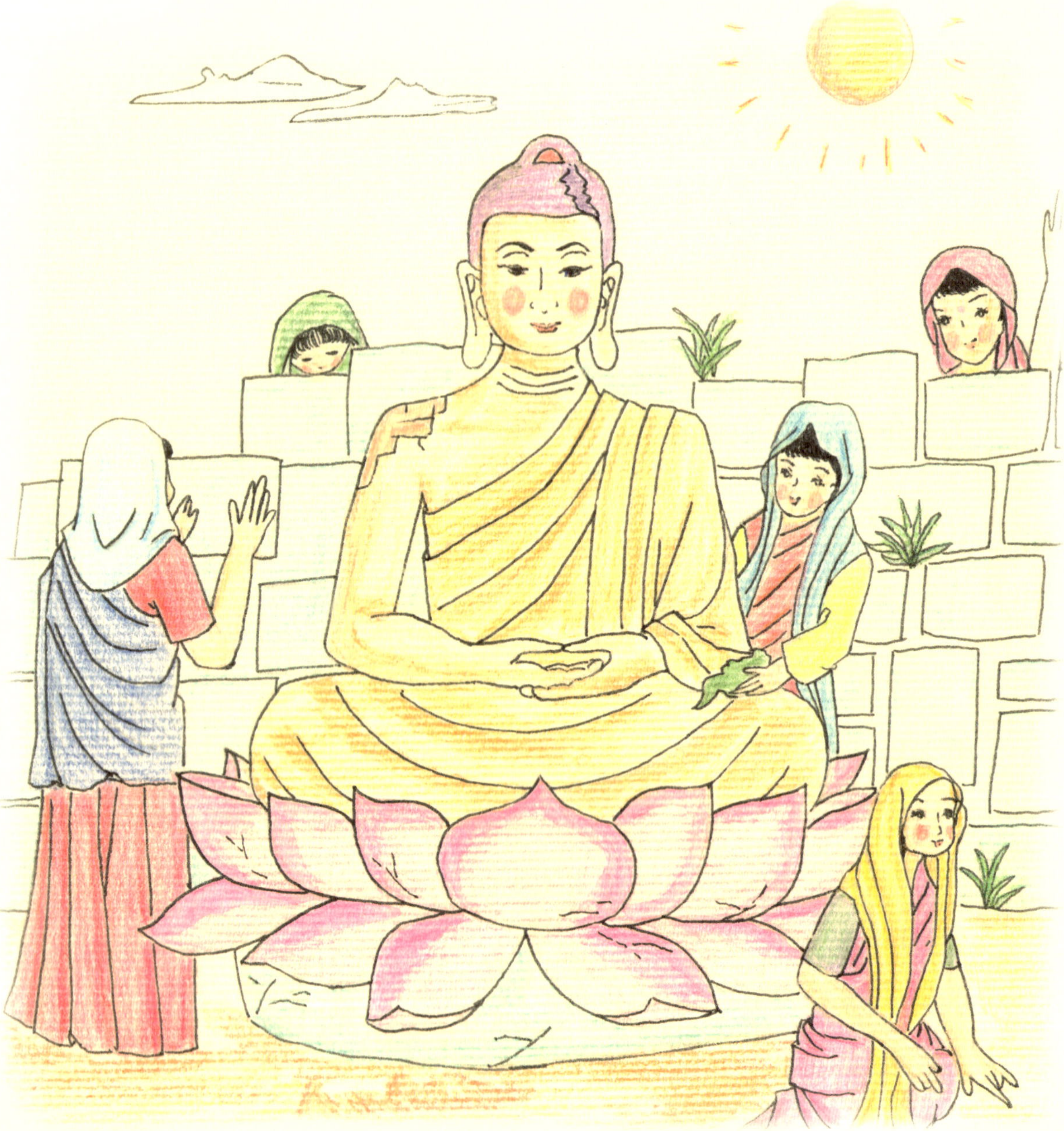

The Thief and the Spider

"Save me! Save me!" Kandata shouted from the hells. Only the Buddha heard him.

Wishing to help him, the Buddha asked, "What did you do to get into the hells?"

"Don't you know? Haven't you heard of me? Why, I was the most famous bandit in the whole wide world. When people heard my name, their hair stood up on end. But now I'm in this hell. It's terrible! If you'll get me out of here, I'll never rob again."

The Buddha asked, "What good did you do in your life?"

Kandata thought, "I've been so cruel, I can't think of anything. I wish I'd done something good."

"I'll take a look into your past lives and find something," said the Buddha. He looked and looked, but he could not find anything. Then he looked back further. "There you are Kandata. It's eons ago, you're walking down a forest path. A spider is crossing the path in front of you. You're stepping aside to keep from hurting it."

Kandata said, "I've always liked spiders. I have no reason to hurt them."

"Because of this one kind deed, I'll help you," said the Buddha and found a tiny spider. He asked the spider to spin a thin thread of gossamer down to the hells.

And so the spider spun a thin thread of gossamer all the way down to the hells and found Kantaka waiting. "Here," said the spider, "take hold of this gossamer and climb up." Taking hold of the gossamer, Kandata said to the spider, "Thanks, little friend, when I get back to earth, I'm going to be the kindest person alive."

Then he began to climb up the thread. Higher and higher he climbed. Suddenly the thread of gossamer began to tremble.

He looked down. Climbing up the thread were thousands of people from the hells. They said to him, "The gossamer is strong enough to hold us all. If we work together, we can escape these hells." More and more people grabbed onto the thread. It stretched and stretched and stretched, but held fast.

Kandata yelled down, "This thread is mine! Let go! Let go! It's mine! It's mine!"

With these words, the gossamer snapped. And Kandata fell plummeting back into the hells with everyone following him. Not even the Buddha could save someone like Kandata.

The Buddha said, "By this, we can see how strong our thoughts are. Kandata's one thought of kindness had the strength of a lifeline. But his one thought of selfishness broke the gossamer."

Never Steal From Your Parents

"There's a feast tomorrow," a woman told her cook. "Kill the fattest sheep and stew it."

The cook went out to the barnyard and spied a fat young sheep with sad eyes grazing under its favorite apple tree. It was a pretty sheep, with curly wool around its ears and a bluish spot on its chest. "Hello, Sad Eyes! This is the last day of your life. Tomorrow you will be the main dish at a grand feast!" The cook said, chuckling as he led the sheep into a pen and tied her up.

There was nothing the cook liked better than lamb stew.

That night the woman had a strange dream. She dreamed that she was flying over the barnyard when she heard the voice of her young daughter, who died many years ago.

"Please don't kill me for the feast tomorrow," the voice cried.

There under the apple tree where her daughter used to play, the woman spotted a young sheep with sad eyes. "I was your daughter in my past life," cried the sheep. "But because I stole many things from you, I've been reborn as a sheep."

When the woman awoke the next morning, she remembered the dream and rushed out to the barnyard to take a look at the sheep. Alas, the sheep pen was empty. "Then it was just a dream," she mumbled and went into the kitchen.

The cook had his knife raised in the air. "Stop! Please don't kill the sheep!" said the woman. Quickly she untied the young sheep and hugged it against her. The wool around the sheep's ears looked like her daughter's hair and the bluish spot on her chest looked like the blue bib that her daughter used to wear.

"But what can we cook for the guests? The sheep is to be the main course," asked the cook.

Just then, a maid came frantically running into the kitchen, "I can't find the long tablecloth. What are we going to do?" she cried.

The woman thought for a minute and said, "Oh, I know where it is!" Forgetting all about the sheep, she ran away with the maid.

Thinking that the woman was insane, the cook went ahead and killed the sheep. When the guests arrived, no one would eat the stew. The poor woman asked, "Why aren't you eating the stew?"

"When we passed by the kitchen on the way in, we saw a sheep head on the table. It looked like your daughter when she was alive. That's why," said one of the guests.

Quickly, the woman ran to the apple tree, but there was no sheep under it. It was just too late!

The Foolish Farmer of Sung

There was a farmer whom we should know
Who lived in Sung a long time ago.
The people in Sung were not very bright.
They didn't know what was wrong from right.

But this farmer was the most foolish of all
From the Indian Ocean to the Great China Wall.
In all the world no one knew
What a foolish thing this farmer would do.

He planted rice and beans in the field
And waited to see what they would yield.
The very first day, not one thing grew.
There was simply nothing the farmer could do.

Day in and day out, he checked on his seeds.
Day in and day out, he pulled up the weeds.
At last came the day he'd been waiting for.
A few sprouts grew, then more and more.

"The earth is all covered with green," said he.
"Soon a bountiful harvest, there will be."
The farmer looked at the plants so small.
"I must help them grow tall."

He worked all day from morning 'til night
And pulled up two inches, every plant in sight.
When he got home, so very tired was he.
Asked his son, "What's the matter with thee?"

"My son," bragged the farmer, "You should know
How hard I've worked to help the new plants grow."
Beaming with pride, the son ran to the field so fast,
Thinking, "My father is wise at last.

He knows how to make plants grow so well.
To all my friends, I'll tell."
But when he got to the field, all he saw.
Were plants withered, dead like straw.

There's a saying in China that all people know.
"Don't be like the farmer, who, a long time ago,

Pulled up the sprouts to make his plants grow."
The moral of the story: let things happen naturally.

The Kind Bear

Once a man went up into the mountains to gather firewood. A heavy storm hit and he lost his way home. He wandered around in the woods looking for the path home. But the more he wandered around the more lost he became. Soon it began to get dark. Clouds covered the stars and the wind blew colder. Night sounds closed in around him—the screech of an owl, the growl of a tiger, the snap of a twig.

The poor man was soaking wet and frightened out of his wits. Suddenly he stumbled upon a cave. Very, very slowly he crawled through the entrance and called out. "Is anyone here?" He stood still and listened. No one answered. There was only silence.

Or was there? What was that noise? A sniff? No, it was the wind. Wait! There it was again.

Hold on! There it was again.

There was no mistake! And it wasn't the wind. It was a sniff and a growl. "Hello!"

"Aaah!" screamed the man, running for the mouth of the cave as if he had wings on his feet. But it was too late. A mighty paw grabbed him and held him high up in the air. A breath of hot air blew into his face. The man froze with fear

"Don't be afraid," said a big bear with eyes as bright as stars. "I won't hurt you. This is my cave and you may stay here out of the storm. Are you hungry? I'll share my berries and honey with you."

Outside the storm was still raging and it was getting colder and colder. Inside the cave, it was dry and warm. Weathering the bear seemed the best choice.

"I-I guess it will be all right," said the man. "Somehow, I feel safe with you. I'll stay." But that night, the man kept one eye open just in case the bear changed his mind and decided to guzzle him up. In spite of himself, he forgot about his fear and soon fell into a peaceful sleep.

The storm raged on for several days so the man stayed on in the cave. Early every morning the bear left the cave and returned at noon with every kind of wonderful berry. There were black berries and blue berries and mulberries and huckleberries and little bits of honeycomb. After the bear and man had eaten, they would sit by the glowing fire and talk late into the night.

The man soon learned that the bear was not only kind, but also very wise. It had many curious things to say about peace among animals and people.

Finally the storm was over and the whole forest was once again alive with the singing of birds. "You can find your way home now," said the bear to the man.

"It's so pleasant here that I forgot about home!" said the man, as he gathered his belongings. "How can I repay your kindness?"

"It did my heart good just to have a friend to talk to," said the bear. "But there is one thing you can do. Don't tell anyone where I live. People kill bears, you know."

"Of course, I won't," said the man and started down the trail. On the way down the mountain, the man ran into a hunter who asked. "Hello, Friend! Have you seen any bear up that way?"

"Yes, a big old bear."

"Oh, where?" asked the hunter, very interested. "A big bear saved my life. But I promised not to tell anyone where it lives."

"Look," said the hunter, "A bear's a bear, just an animal—only good for food. We're people and we need meat to stay alive. What good is that bear going to do you now? I'll tell you what. You tell me where it lives and I'll give you enough fur for a nice warm coat."

"A fur coat surely would be warm," said the man, looking at his old tattered coat. "But I don't think it would be right. That bear was good to me."

"And I'll give you half the meat. No matter what, you have to eat," said the hunter. "It'd be a shame to let that bear go."

"You're right about that," said the man, feeling hungry. "It would be a shame. But a promise is a promise. Good day, friend, I must be on my way." And off he went, cold and hungry, but happy.

Lion's Milk

At the time of the Buddha, there were four sons whose father had died and left them all his wealth. One day they paid the Buddha a visit. "The four of us can't agree on who should get what," said the oldest brother. "All day long we bicker and quarrel over this and that. What should we do?"

"Listen while I tell you a story," said the Buddha.

Once there was a king who became ill. The doctor said to him, 'You will die unless you take medicine made from lion's milk."

The king was disturbed. "Where can I get lion's milk?" he asked. "There isn't any in the palace." So he sent a decree throughout

73

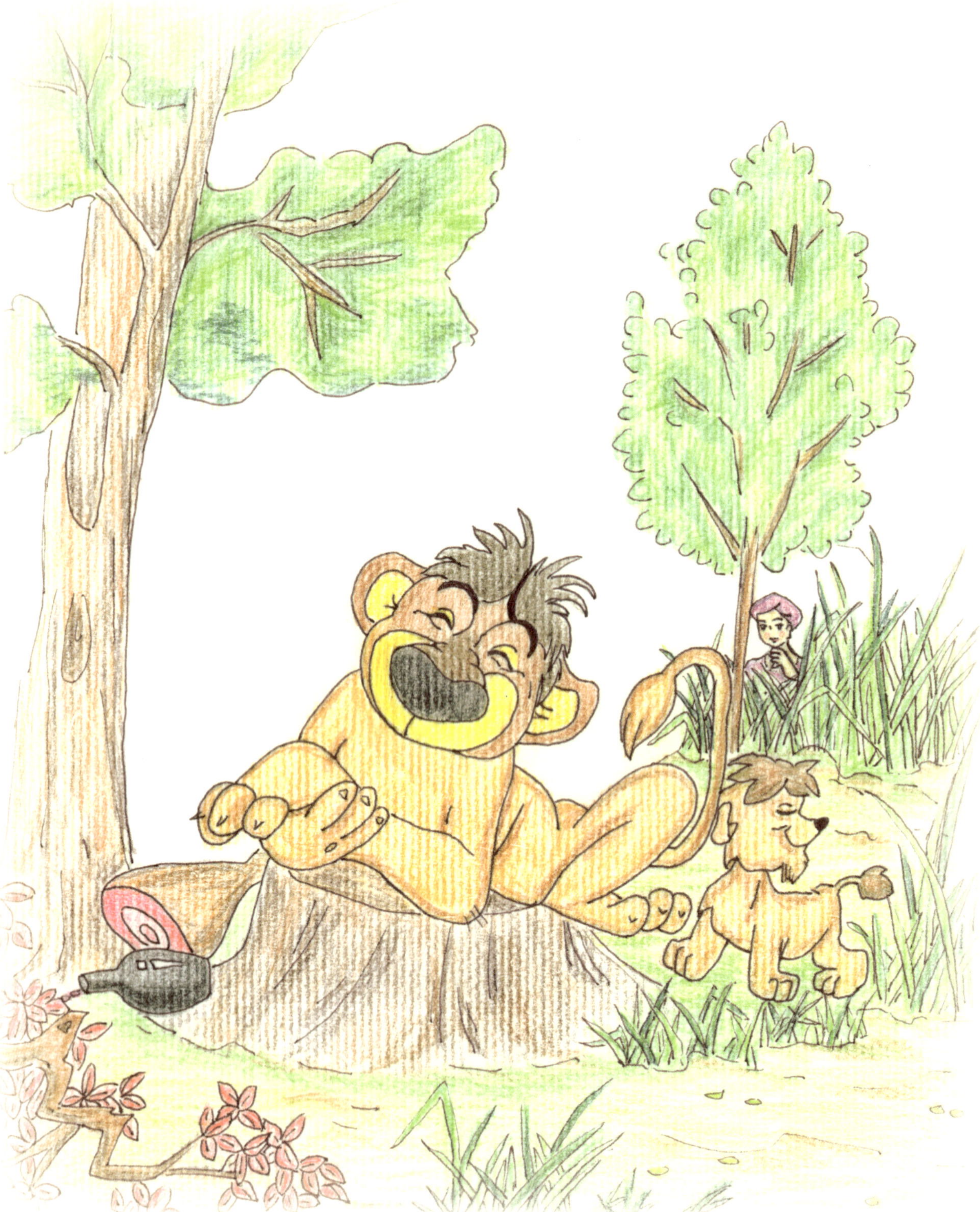

the land that whoever brought him lion's milk will be given half his kingdom.

In the woods nearby lived a poor hunter. When he heard the king's offer, he said, "I know where to get lion's milk. Soon I will be a very rich man!"

The next day he went high up into the mountains to where he knew there was a lion's den. He set out some wine and raw meat, then he hid. Before long, a big lioness came and hungrily ate the meat and drank the wine.

She became so drunk and sleepy that she lay down for a nap. That was just what the hunter had hoped for. Quickly, he milked the lion before she awakened.

Happily, he went back down the mountain with the lion's milk.

Along the way, he came to a small inn where he decided to spend the night. Being very tired, he soon fell into a deep sleep.
Later that night, an Arhat came along the same road and spent the night under an oak tree next to the inn.

As he sat in meditation, he could see and hear everything that happened in the inn. He could even see into the hunter's dream.

The hunter's legs were boasting. They said, "If I hadn't walked up the mountain, the hunter never could have gotten the lion's milk. I'm the one who did it!"

His arms argued with his legs, "If I hadn't milked the lion, he never would have gotten the milk out. I'm really the responsible one!"

His ears joined the argument. They said, "Listen, it all began with me. If I hadn't heard that the king needed lion's milk, he would've never gone to hunt for a lioness."

His eyes said, "Look, if I didn't see, none of you could have done anything."

His tongue spoke up at this point, "Silence, all of you. The merit will lie with me, you'll see."

At this, the legs, hands, eyes and ears became enraged against the tongue. They made such a fuss that it woke up the hunter.

He quickly grabbed the lion's milk, thinking, "But I'm the one who has the milk," he thought, recalling his dream. And he hurried to the palace and gave the milk to the king. "How did you get the milk?" asked the happy king.

"It was easy," said the hunter, bragging. "I tricked the lioness into going to sleep, then I milked her."

His tongue, waiting for this moment, burst out, "That's not lion's milk. That's donkey's milk!"

The king believed the tongue and was enraged at being tricked, "You come to waste my time with donkey's milk! You shall be executed!" he cried. The poor hunter didn't know what to do.

Suddenly, a bright light filled the room and the Arhat appeared and said, "Your majesty, the milk that the hunter brought is really lion's milk. Last night, I spent the night near an inn. This is what happened..." he told the whole story to the king.

The king gave in and said, "I believe your story. Have the medicine prepared with the lion's milk." After drinking the medicine, he became well. He kept his promise and gave the hunter a kingdom to rule.

When the Buddha finished the story, he said to the four brothers, "You see, it's not just brothers who fight among themselves. Even bodies fight and cause trouble."

The brothers understood the message. "We'll stop this useless quarreling among ourselves and quit being so selfish," they said. The story goes on that the brothers decided to give their wealth to the poor and to become disciples of the Buddha. Having given up their selfish ways, they quickly became Arhats.

The Buddha told another story about the brothers. At the time of a Buddha named Mwo Wen, Shariputra was then a monk and the four brothers offered him a kashya. That is why they were able to leave the home life and become Arhats so quickly.

A kashya is a large sash made of seven strips of cloth that are sewn together. It is worn over the shoulder of a Buddhist monk or nun. The strips of cloth are shaped like fields. So the kashya is known as a "field of blessings."

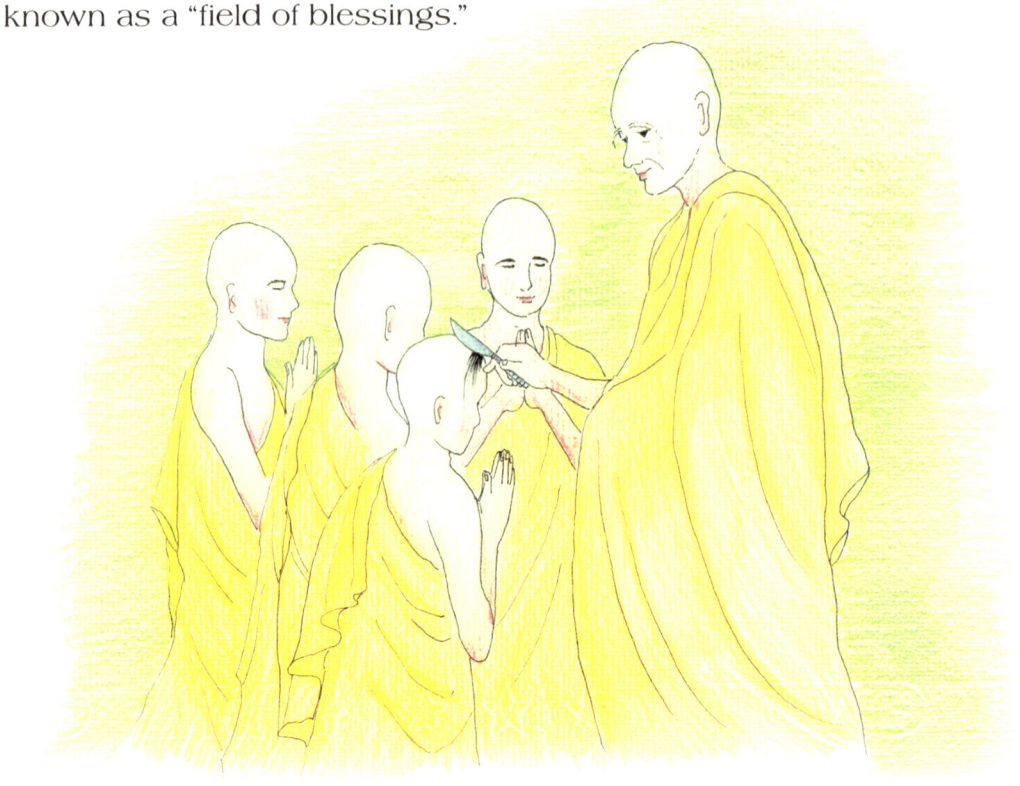

The Snake and the Seven Pots of Gold

Thousands of years ago, a rich man lived in the countryside, not far from a city. He had seven pots of gold. His gold was more precious to him than anything else in the world. Everyday he came to check on his gold and count it. There was nothing he loved more than the sounds of coins clinking together.

He had no friends and when his neighbors came by to look in on him, he would chase them away. "Get away from here!" he shouted. "All you want is my gold." So they stayed away.

But one day the man fell ill. To part with enough gold to pay a doctor was unbearable for him. So he wasted away and died.

After his death, he was reborn as a snake and returned to guard the pots of gold. So fiercely did the snake guard the gold, that the most clever of thieves dared not enter the gold cellar.

And when the snake died, it was again reborn as a snake returned to guard the pots of gold. The same thing happened in the next life, and in the next life, and so on. But in one lifetime, the snake thought. What's the big deal? All I do is guard gold? Is this all there is to life? I am sick and tired of this. And the snake that once loved gold, began to loathe gold. "I must find my own treasure and have some adventure in life," it said. So, out the window, through the gate, and onto the road it slithered.

There were people walking and pushing carts, men on camels and horses, ladies riding in carriages, children on donkeys, and dogs barking. And all of them were going merrrily along their way to and from the city. It was the most excitement the snake had ever seen.

"Please someone, take me with you. I want to see the city, it hissed. The snake felt a warm hand on its neck. A young man gently picked it up and slipped it into a sack. Then off to the city they went.

On the way, they passed by a traveler. "Good morning, friend!" greeted the traveler. The young man nodded his head. For he was mute and could not speak.

Now, the snake, not knowing the man was mute, thought, "Why doesn't he answer? How rude!" And the snake got a little mad, as snakes are known to do. Further on down the road, they passed by a family. "Hello! Hello!" the family sang out. The man waved and smiled, and the snake in the sack couldn't see him. All it knew was, the man didn't speak.

"The nerve of this man! What's he so stuck-up about?" The snake was really mad by now. "He deserves to be bitten!" said the snake, hissing and flicking its long evil tongue.

But wait a minute! The snake didn't want to lose its ride. This wasn't the right time to get mad. So it held its temper, stuck its head back in the sack, and cooled down.

On down the road, they met a jolly old man. "Where are you headed?" he asked. The young man pointed to the city.

Hearing no answer from the man, the snake in the bag thought, "What? Not again! I need to teach this man some manners. Ride or no ride!" And the snake coiled up, ready to strike. It was so mad.

Then "thunk", the moment before the deadly strike, the young man gently plopped the sack down on the steps of a temple and opened it. The snake was face to face with the young man.

The young man smiled and said hello with his fingers. Realizing that the young man could not speak, the snake almost bit its own tongue off. "N-nice day," the snake said weakly and slid slowly back down into the sack.

So kind were the eyes of the young man that the snake forgot about being mad. In fact it felt a little ashamed. And that was hard for a snake.

A wrinkled old monk with bright eyes came and took the snake inside the temple. The snake had never seen anything so beautiful—the golden Buddha images, the lamps and flowers. He wanted to stay in the temple forever.

The old monk said, "In your past life, you were a miser who hoarded his gold. Because of that, you were reborn as a snake. Now I can see that you have lost your love for gold and dislike being a snake." "Right! But how can I get out of being reborn as a snake again! Enough is enough."

"You can make offerings to the temple and share your gold with the poor."

"No problem, that gold is of no use to me. Is that all?"

"You need to get rid of your anger. You almost bit my friend."

"Yeah, I almost blew it," said the snake. "I'm really sorry about that. Where is he anyway? I want to thank him. If I ever get reborn as a person, I'd like to be like him." The snake looked for the young man everywhere, but could not find him.

The monks kept the snake at the temple as a guard. That made the snake very happy. And as far as snakes go, it turned into as gentle and kind as a snake could be. "Snakes bring good fortune," said the people when they saw it slithering through the grass.

By and by, the snake died. It was reborn as a god in the Heaven of the Thirty-Three. After that, the god was reborn as Shariputra, the disciple of the Buddha who was foremost in wisdom.

The Upside-down Dragon

Once there was an Arhat who flew around in a big bell that was shaped like a bowl. Long ropes with tassels were wrapped around the bell.

Sometimes, the Arhat would fly down to the bottom of the river to speak Dharma for the Dragon King who lived there. He followed the custom of the Buddha by accepting an offering of food before he spoke. When he returned to the temple where he lived, he would have a young novice wash his bowl.

One day a few scraps of food were left in the bowl and the novice secretly ate them. He said, "This is the most delicious food I've ever tasted. I'm going to follow my teacher next time and see if I can get a whole bowl of it."

So the next time the Arhat went to the dragon palace, the young novice hid under the bell and held onto the ropes. The Dragon King just so happened to see him hanging onto the ropes when the Arhat landed. The King said, "I see that I have two visitors today. Who is your little friend?"

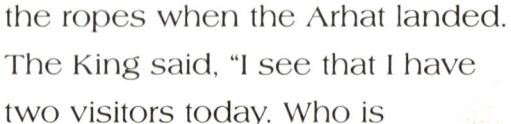

When the Arhat saw the novice hiding behind the bell, he apologized. "It's a mistake. I didn't know he was with me."

84

The Dragon King very graciously said to the novice, "You're welcome this time. But you must never come back here again!"

Then with pomp and majesty, the Dragon King seated the novice at a large crystal table spread with a banquet of delicious food of every kind—rice and honey, stews and curries, lemon cakes and strawberry cremes, mangoes and sweet melons. The novice had a huge appetite and ate everything that was on the table, his heart singing with joy. As soon as he finished, he went to thank the Dragon King. But he had disappeared.

Being curious, the novice strolled into a garden where beautiful flowers were blooming and celestial music was playing. In the garden were hundreds of exquisite female dragons swaying and turning with the music. One was lovelier than the next. The novice was dazzled by such beauty. "I would like to be a dragon," he said to himself. Just then he heard the Arhat ring the bell and knew it was time to leave.

Back at the temple, the memory of the dragon palace stayed with the novice. He went around chanting to himself, "I vow to be reborn as a dragon." And when he sat in meditation, he concentrated very hard on becoming a dragon.

One night while sitting in meditation, he was concentrating so well that he could see through the walls of the temple. There on the other side of the wall hidden behind a grove of trees was a large pool. "This must be a dragon pool," he thought.

The next day he found the pool exactly where he thought it was. "At last I can become a dragon," he cried, pulling his robe over his head. Then jumping into the pool, he drowned. And sure enough, he was reborn as a dragon.

He was a huge dragon and handsome as well. The other dragons made him their Dragon King. And he reigned supremely in his dragon palace under water.

When the other monks learned what had happened to the novice, they called him the "upside-down dragon." They were very sorry that he had become a dragon and had thus delayed his chance to become a Buddha. They knew that as an animal, he would have to undergo suffering. When they passed by the pool they could see the huge dragon swimming below in the clear, green water. But the dragon ignored them. He was quite happy with the lot he had chosen.

How People Came to be on Earth

When the planet earth was very, very new, there were no human beings on it. There was no sun, moon, or stars. There was no day or night, no years or months, and no spring, summer, autumn, or winter.

At one time, some gods from the Light-sound Heaven flew down to the earth. They did not eat food like people do. When they got hungry, they only had to think happy thoughts and they would be full.

Their bodies were made of light. As they flew through the darkness down to earth, it looked as if the sky was filled with thousands of fireflies flitting and darting about.

The Gods Began to Eat

"The earth is very beautiful but strange," said the gods, hovering over the planet. "Look, there's something shiny and greenish-blue on the ground. We've never seen anything so wonderful!"

"I'm going to taste it!" said one fun-loving god, sticking his fingers in the greenish-blue stuff, "Oh, it's so sweet!"

Playfully, the other light gods stuck their fingers in the stuff and tasted it, too. Their little lights blinked off and on. "This is delicious. Let's have some more," they cried with delight.

"We can't stop eating!" The gods said playfully as they ate more and more. They called it the fat of the land.

Now that the gods were eating the fat of the land, their light and delicate bodies began to get heavy and plump. They could no longer fly. They had to walk on the ground but they didn't care. "Eating the fat of the land is better than having happy thoughts," they said among themselves.

By and by, the gods lost all their beautiful lights, but no one noticed. They forgot how to be curious and playful, but no one noticed. "We'll call ourselves people," they said. All they cared about was eating their fill. And greed came to be.

The gods in the heavens looked down and said, "The light gods have lost their light. We must send them help."

So the gods placed the sun, moon, and stars in the sky above them. Earth began to rotate on its axis and day and night came to be. The moon began to revolve around the earth and the months came to be. The earth began to revolve around the sun and the years passed by.

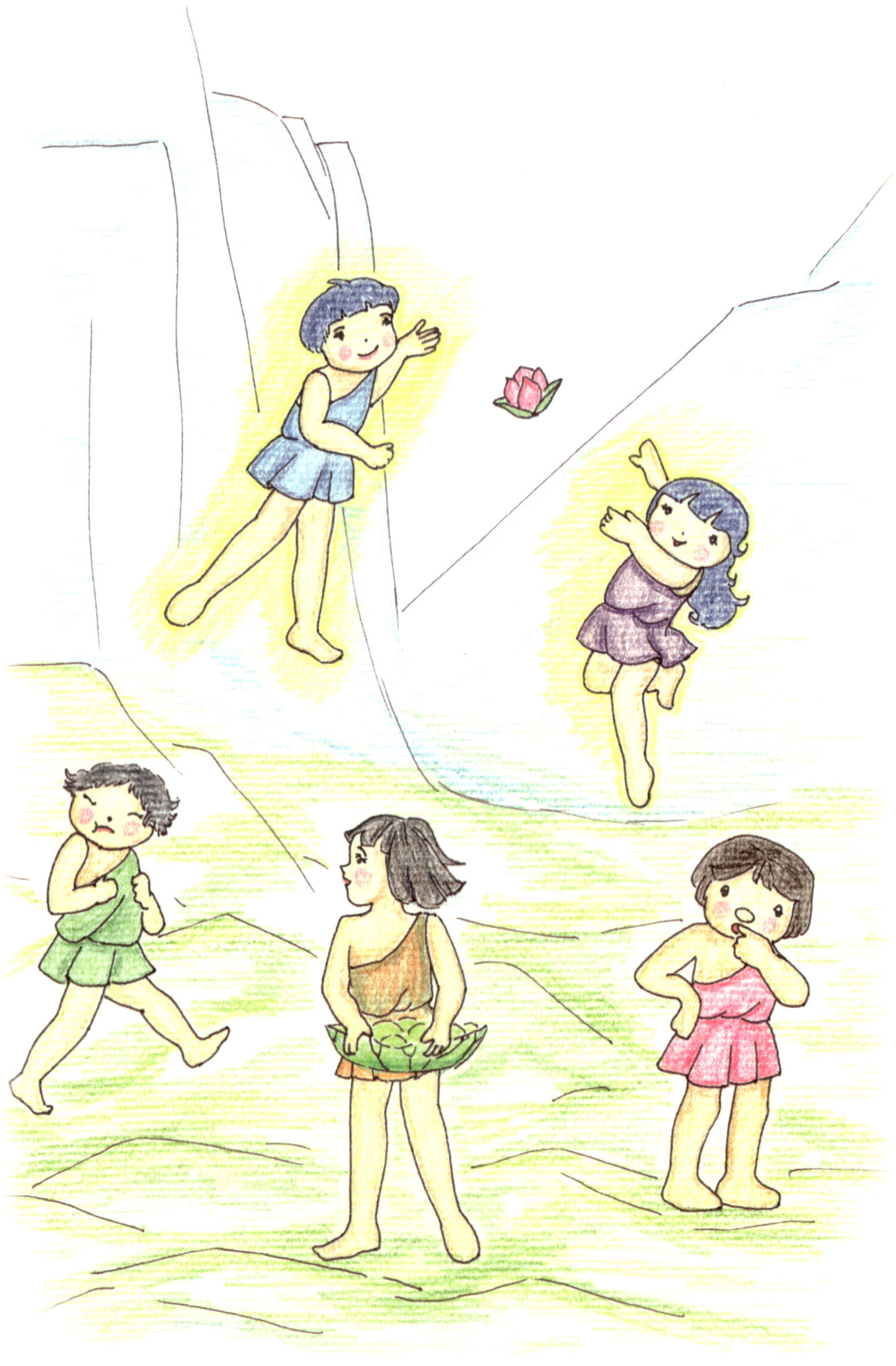

The light gods became so human that they forgot they were ever gods. The ones who ate the most fat of the land became ugly. Those who ate less kept some of their godlike beauty. The beautiful ones snubbed the ugly ones and said, "You're just jealous because we are more beautiful than you!" Jealousy and arrogance came to be.

One cried, "Look! There isn't any more fat of the land. It has all disappeared! Whose fault is it?" Everyone blamed everyone else. Quarreling came to be.

Then some new fat of the land grew on the earth. The gods tasted it and said, "It's not as sweet as the other, but it's still delicious."

Again, the ones who ate the most became uglier and fatter. And the ones who ate less kept some of their godlike beauty. This caused even more jealousy and quarreling. Fighting came to be.

Then all the fat of the land disappeared again. Another kind of fat of the land began to grow on earth. "It isn't as sweet as the other two, but it's still delicious," said the gods, tasting it.

And the gods became even more ugly and fat and more fighting broke out. Soon all that fat of the land disappeared. And no more grew in its place.

By and by, a new food called grain grew on earth. Once the gods began to eat the grain, they changed into men and women. If a woman liked a man, she would take him food. She became his wife and he became her husband.

When the gods first came to earth, they lived in the open air. Now that there were men and women, they built shelters to live in. Husbands and wives began to live together and have children.

A Lazy Idea

When the people were hungry, they would go out and eat enough grain to satisfy themselves. But then one day, someone had a lazy thought, "If we collect enough food and store it, I won't have to go look for food every time I'm hungry."

When the others saw what the lazy one was doing, they said, "That's a smart idea!"

Soon everyone was gathering enough food for two or three days, then for weeks at a time. Before, only a little grain was picked every day, so it quickly grew back. But now that the people were picking large amounts at one time, it all disappeared.

Another kind of grain grew in this place. It was covered with hulls and had to be threshed and cooked. It didn't grow as fast as the other grain. And it was not as delicious.

The people said, "Let's divide the land into fields and find ways to make it grow faster." This was the beginning of farming. People began to think in terms of "this is mine and that is yours".

"Someone has taken all the grain from my field!" shouted a farmer one day. Stealing came to be.

The stealing brought about more fighting. No one could decide who was right or wrong.

"We need someone to settle our quarrels," the people said. They chose the men who were still godlike to lead them. The men became kings and were given kingdoms to rule.

At first, all the kings were kind and just and ruled fairly. But then some kings became mean and cruel and took the people as their slaves.

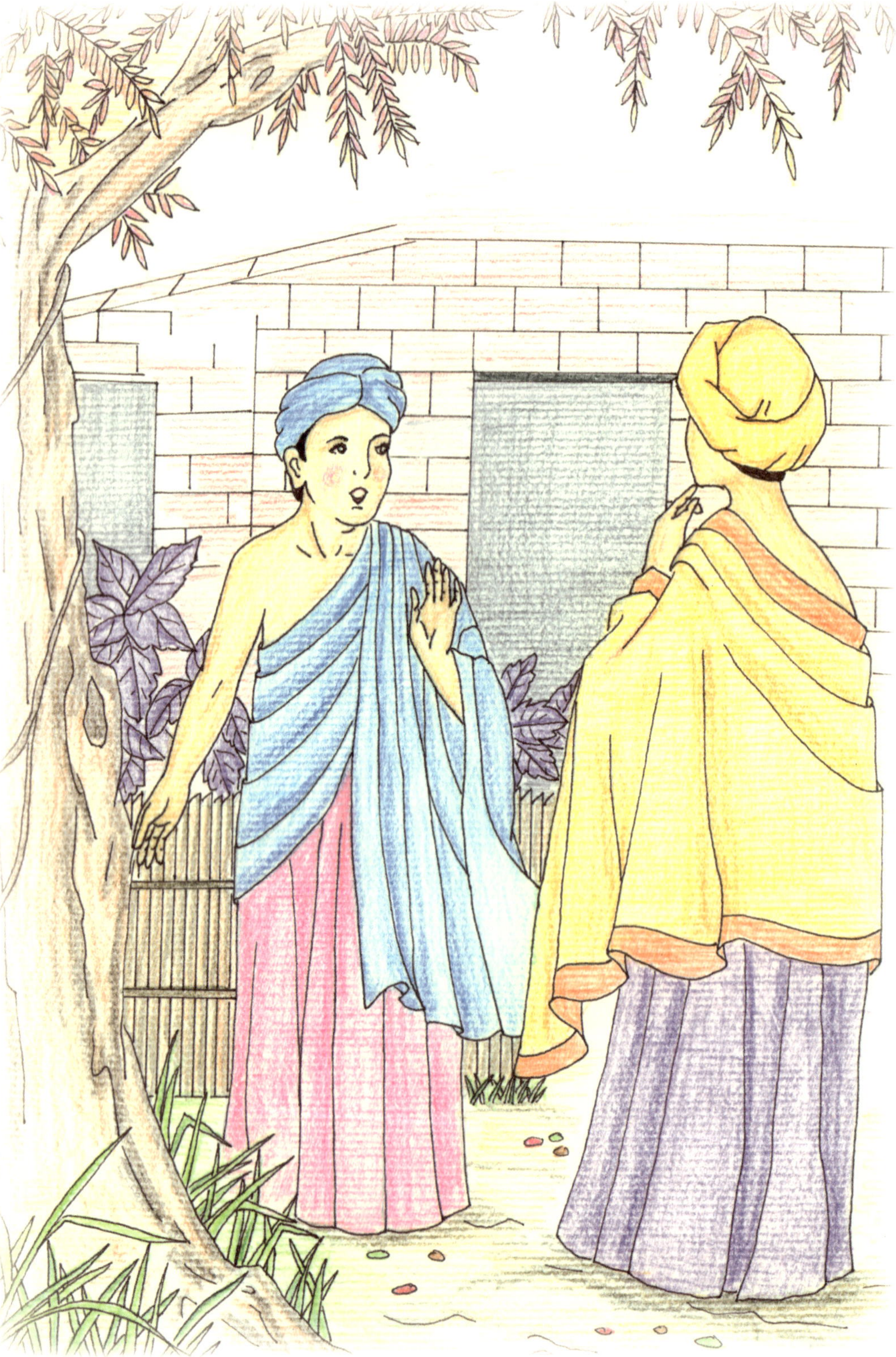

The Life-span Gets Shorter

The average life of a person was 84,000 years, but when people began to steal and fight, the life span dropped to 40,000 years. Then with more greed and fighting, the life span dropped to 10,000 years.

Until then the people only stole and fought, but no one had told a lie. One day, a man was accused of stealing and brought before a king. "Did you steal? the king asked.

"No," said the man.

He didn't want to get punished. So lying came to be. Once the people started lying, their life span dropped down to 1,000 years.

Lying led to double-tongued speech that led to harsh speech and gossip. Life spans dropped to 500 years. No one knew right from wrong any longer.

Shakyamuni Buddha Enters the World

When people's life span reached an average of 100 years, Shakyamuni Buddha appeared in the world. That was over 3,000 years ago. The Buddha brought the Proper Dharma into the world and taught kindness and compassion to purify the hearts of the people. If they had listened to him, their life spans would have increased, but few listened.

The Future

The Dharma that the Buddha taught will gradually leave the world. People will do worse things and their life span will get even shorter. Every 100 years, their life span will get shorter by one year. In time, it would be only ten years.

The earth will not be beautiful as it is now. The food will not be delicious and good to eat. There will be no trees, only stones and boulders and shrubs. And there will no gold, silver, or jewels.

People Bring Forth True Hearts

Then some people with good hearts will say, "We should stop killing each other. It's not right." Once killing stops, the life span will increase to 20 years.

Other good people will say, "If we keep on stealing, no one will be safe. We should stop stealing." Once stealing stops, the life span will increase to 40 years.

Then husbands and wives will decide to live together in peace and take good care of their children. The life span will increase to 80 years. And once people stop lying, the life span will be 160 years.

When people stop talking behind each other's backs, the life span will increase to 320 years. And when they speak with kindness in their hearts, the life span will be up to 640 years.

When gossiping stops, people's life span will increase to 10,000 years. And when jealousy is forgotten, the life span will be 20,000 years.

When people respect their parents and take care of them in their old age, the life span will be 80,000 years. Everyone will be happy and healthy. Only seven diseases will remain.

1. People may get cold.
2. People may get hot.
3. People may get hungry.
4. People may feel thirsty.
5. People may have desire.
6. People may eat too much.
7. People will still eventually get old.

Maitreya Buddha

The world will be more beautiful than it is now. Sparkling lakes, enchanted forests, and fragrant flowers will adorn the land. The food will be delicious and there will be exquisite clothing and precious jewels for everyone. People will be good friends with each other and live in perfect peace. Mosquitoes, flies and other poisonous creatures will have disappeared.

At that time Maitreya Buddha will appear in the world. The people will honor him and make offerings of flower garlands and sweet-smelling incense. Peace and joy will spread throughout the land.

Then after 84,000 years have passed, people will begin to become greedy again and their life spans will decrease. The whole cycle will be repeated, over and over again.

GLOSSARY

ARHAT- One of the stages of enlightenment. It has three meanings, which are: 1. Worthy of offerings
2. Killer of evil
3. Will not be reborn

ASURAS- Beings who have spiritual powers, but no blessings. The men are ugly. They like to fight and drink wine. The women are beautiful and like to cause trouble. Asuras can appear as people or animals.

BANYAN TREE- A sacred tree in India. Roots ascend from its branches, take root in the soil and become trunks. There can be as many as 200 trunks that encompass a 900 ft. circle.

BHIKSHU- An ordained monk.

BODHI TREE- A sacred tree under which Shakyamuni Buddha became enlightened.

BODHISATTVA- A compassionate being that enlightens himself and helps others to be enlightened.

BUDDHA DHARMA- The teachings of the Buddha.

CULTIVATE- To develop wisdom and compassion by following the teachings of the Buddha.

CULTIVATOR- One who cultivates the Buddha Dharma through practice.

DHARMA- A rule or method; the teaching of the Buddha.

DHARMA MASTER- A polite term to address a teacher of the Dharma.

ENLIGHTENMENT- Understanding the truth of life, freedom from ignorance and desire.

FULL LOTUS- A meditation posture with both legs crossed over each other and resting on the thighs.

GILD- To paint with gold.

JETA GROVE- A monastery in Shravasti given to the Buddha by the merchant Sudatta.

JATAKA TALES- Stories of the past lives of the Buddha.

KARMA- "Action" or the law of cause and effect. For every action there is a cause. Good actions lead one closer to perfect happiness or Nirvana; bad actions lead one away.

LAYPERSON- A Buddhist who is not a nun or monk.

LEAVE HOME- To renounce the home like and devote oneself to the Buddha Dharma.

LOTUS FLOWER- A symbol of enlightenment.

MANTRA- A symbolic phrase made of harmonious sounds that is chanted or recited.

MEDITATION- Sitting quietly to focus the mind for inner calmness and peace.

MONASTERY- A place where monks nuns, live, study, and worship.

NIRVANA- A state of everlasting joy and peace attained by enlightened sages.

OFFERING BOWL- A bowl in which nuns and monks collect offerings of food.

ORDAINED- To take the full precepts to become a monk or nun.

PRATYEKA BUDDHA- A hermit who is self enlightened.

PRECEPTS- Rules of conduct given by the Buddha to his disciples. The Five Precepts are: no killing, no stealing, no sexual misconduct, no false speech, and no intoxicants

REBIRTH- The belief that one is reborn in a different body after death.

RECITING- Half-singing, half-speaking sacred phrases or texts; very calming and peaceful.

SAMADHI- A state of deep meditation in which one gains insight.

SANGHA- The community of Buddhist nuns and monks.

SANSKRIT- An ancient Indian language. Many sacred Buddhist books were written in Sanskrit.

SHARIRA- The remains of a part of the body or something left behind by a holy person.

SPIRITUAL PENETRATIONS- The power to see future and past lives and to transform oneself into various forms.

SUTRAS- Truths spoken by the Buddha and his disciples under the Buddha's direction.

TANG DYNASTY- From 618 AD to 905 AD. A time when Buddhism flourished in China.

TRANSLATE- To put in a different language.

TRAYASTRIMSA HEAVEN- The second of the six heavens in the realm of desire.

TUSHITA HEAVEN- The first of the six heavens of desire.

The Dharma Realm Buddhist Association

The Dharma Realm Buddhist Association (DRBA) was founded in the United States of America in 1959 by the Venerable Master Hsuan Hua (prior to his own arrival in the U.S.) to bring the genuine teachings of the Buddha to the entire world.

Its goals are to propagate the Proper Dharma, to translate the Mahayana Buddhist scriptures into the world's languages and to promote ethical education.

The members of the association guide themselves with six ideals established by the Venerable Master which are:
no fighting, no greed, no seeking, no selfishness, no pursuing personal advantage, and no lying.

They hold in mind the credo:

>Freezing, we do not scheme.
>Starving, we do not beg.
>Dying of poverty, we ask for nothing.
>According with conditions, we do not change.
>Not changing, we accord with conditions.
>We adhere firmly to our three great principles.
>We renounce our lives to do the Buddha's work.
>We take responsibility in molding our own destinies.
>We rectify our lives to fulfill our role
>>as members of the Sangha.

> Encountering specific matters,
> > we understand the principles.
> Understanding the principles,
> > we apply them in specific matters.
> We carry on the single pulse of
> > the patriarchs' mind-transmission.

During the following decades, international Buddhist communities such as Gold Mountain Monastery, the City of Ten Thousand Buddhas, the City of the Dharma Realm and various other branch facilities were founded. All these operate under the traditions of the Venerable Master and through the auspices of the Dharma Realm Buddhist Association.

Following the guidelines of Shakyamuni Buddha, the Sangha members in these monastic facilities maintain the practices of taking only one meal a day and of always wearing their precept sashes. Reciting the Buddha's name, studying the teachings, and practicing meditation, they dwell together in harmony and personally put into practice the Buddha's teachings.

Reflecting Master Hua's emphasis on translation and education, the Association also sponsors an International Translation Institute, vocational training programs for Sangha and laity, Dharma Realm Buddhist University, and elementary and secondary schools.

The Way-places of this Association are open to sincere individuals of all races, religions, and nationalities.

Everyone who is willing to put forth his/her best effort in nurturing humaneness, righteousness, merit, and virtue in order to understand the mind and see the nature is welcome to join in the study and practice.

Venerable Master Hsuan Hua
The Founder of
Dharma Realm Buddhist Association

The Venerable Master Hsuan Hua was also known as An Tse and To Lun. The name Hsuan Hua was bestowed upon him after he received the transmission of the Wei Yang Lineage of the Chan School from Venerable Elder Hsu Yun. He left the home life at the age of nineteen.

After the death of his mother, he lived in a tiny thatched hut by her grave-side for three years, as an act of filial respect. During that time, he practiced meditation and studied the Buddha's teachings. Among his many practices were eating only once a day at midday and never lying down to sleep.

In 1948 the Master arrived in Hong Kong, where he founded the Buddhist Lecture Hall and other monasteries. In 1962 he brought the Proper Dharma to America and the West, where he lectured extensively on the major works of the Mahayana Buddhist canon and established the Dharma Realm Buddhist Association, as well as the City of Ten Thousand Buddhas, the International Translation Institute, various other monastic facilities, Dharma Realm Buddhist University, Developing Virtue Secondary School, Instilling Goodness Elementary school, the vocational Sangha and Laity Training Programs, and other education centers.

The Master passed into stillness on June 7, 1995, in Los Angeles,

U.S.A., causing many people throughout the world to mourn the sudden setting of the sun of wisdom. Although he has passed on, his lofty example will always be remembered. Throughout his life he worked selflessly and vigorously to benefit the people of the world and all living beings. His wisdom and compassion inspired many to correct their faults and lead wholesome lives.

Here we include the Records of the Mendicant of Chang Bai written by the Venerable Master to serve as a model for all of us to emulate.

> The Mendicant of Chang Bai was simple
>   and honest in nature.
> He was always quick to help people and benefit others.
> Forgetting himself for the sake of the Dharma,
>   he was willing to sacrifice his life.
> Bestowing medicines according to people's illnesses,
>   he offered his own marrow and skin.
> His vow was to unite in substance with millions of beings.
> His practice exhausted empty space as
>   he gathered in the myriad potentials,
> Without regard for past, future, or present;
> With no distinctions of north, south, east, or west.

Namo Dharma Protector Wei Tuo Bodhisattva

Verse of Transference

May the merit and virtue accrued from this work

Adorn the Buddhas' Pure Lands,

Repaying the four kinds of kindness above

And aiding those suffering in the paths below.

May those who see and hear of this

All bring forth the resolve for Bodhi

And, when this retribution body is over,

Be born together in the Land of Ultimate Bliss.

Commentary on Buddhist Sutras

by Ven. Master Hua's

	Price US
Amitabha Sutra	$8.00
Dharma Flower (Lotus) Sutra (1 set, 10 books)	$79.50
The Wonderful Dharma Lotus Flower Sutra (Vol. 11-16)	@$10.00
Flower Adornment (Avatamsaka) Sutra (1 set, 22 books)	$174.50
Flower Adornment (Avatamsaka) Sutra Prologue (1set, 4 books)	$38.00
Heart Sutra & Verses Without a Stand	$7.50
Medicine Master Sutra	$10.00
Shurangama Sutra	$59.50
Shurangama Sutra, Vol.8:The Fifty Skandha-Demon States	$20.00
Great Strength Bodhisattva's Perfect Penetration	$5.00
Shastra on the Door to Understanding the Hundred Dharmas	$6.50
Sixth Patriarch Sutra (hardcover)	$15.00
Sixth Patriarch Sutra (softcover)	$10.00
Sutra In Forty-two Sections	$5.00
Sutra of the Past Vows of Earth Store Bodhisattva (hardcover, commentary)	$16.00
Song of Enlightenment	$5.00
Vajra Prajna Paramita (Diamond) Sutra	$8.00
Sutra of the Past Vows of Earth Store Bodhisattva (softcover, sutra text only)	$5.00

Flower Adornment (Avatamsaka) Sutra
A Basic Explanation by Venerable Master Hua

Known as the "King of Kings" of all Buddhist scriptures because of its profundity and great length (81 rolls containing more than 700,000 Chinese characters), this Sutra contains the most complete explanation of the Buddha's state and the Bodhisattva's quest for Awakening.

****

Dharma Flower (Lotus) Sutra
A Basic Explanation by Venerable Master Hua

In this Sutra, which was spoken during the last period of the Buddha's teaching, the Buddha proclaims the ultimate principles of the Dharma, which unite all previous teachings into one. The entire work comprises sixteen volumes.

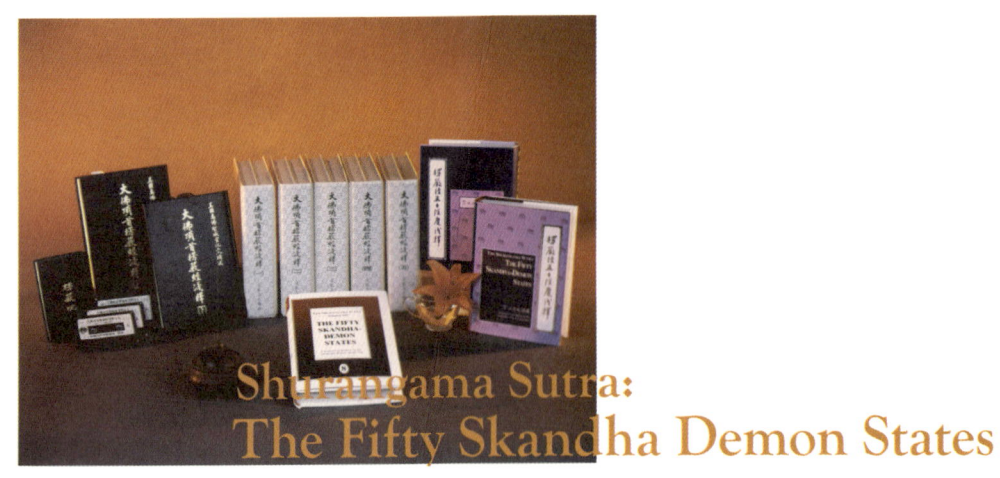

Shurangama Sutra: The Fifty Skandha Demon States
A Basic Explanation by Venerable Master Hua

A bilingual (Chinese/English) edition of Venerable Master Hua's commentary on the final section of the Shurangama Sutra (volume eight of the English only edition). Essential reading for anyone who practices meditation or who wishes to follow a spiritual teacher.

****

Sutra of the Past Vows of Earth Store Bodhisattva
A Basic Explanation by Venerable Master Hua

This Sutra tells how Earth Store Bodhisattva (Kshitigarbha) attained his position among the greatest Bodhisattvas as the Foremost in Vows. It also explains the workings of karma, how beings undergo rebirth, and the various kinds of hells. This is the first English translation.

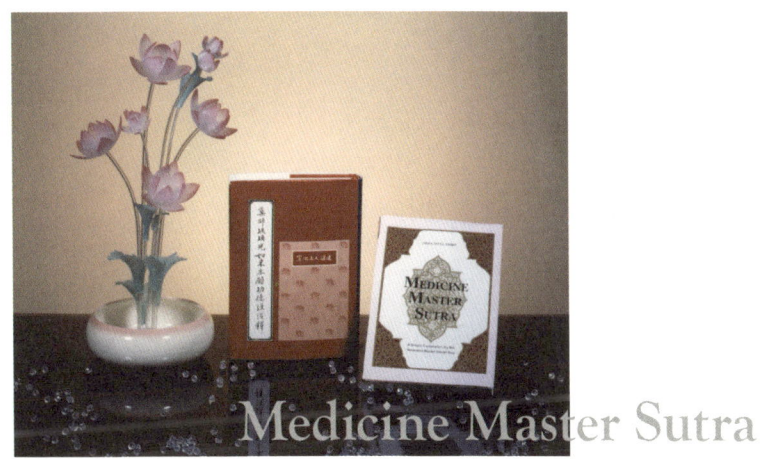

Medicine Master Sutra
A Basic Explanation by Venerable Master Hua

This Sutra describes Medicine Master (Akshobhya) Vaidurya Light Thus Come One's twelve great vows, the benefits derived from hearing this sutra, how to worship the Buddha and uphold the sutra, tand the benefits derived from worshipping.

****

Sixth Patriarch's Sutra
A Basic Explanation by Venerable Master Hua

One of the foremost scriptures of Ch'an Buddhism, this text describes the life and teachings of the remarkable Patriarch of the T'ang Dynasty, Great Master Hui Neng, who, though unable to read or write, was enlightened.

In Memory of the Venerable Master Hsüan Hua

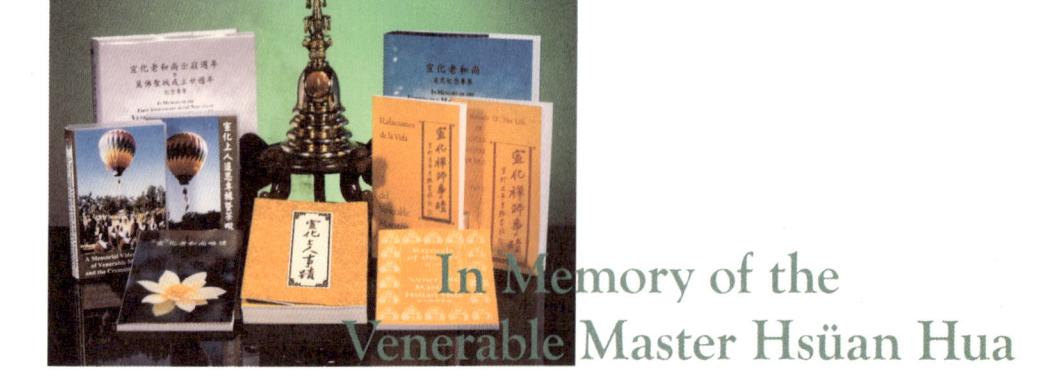

Compiled following Master Hua's "completion of the stillness" on June 7, 1995, these books contain photos of the Master and records of programs he founded as well as biographical accounts of the Master's life, essays, and poems written by the Master's disciples and others whose lives he touched. Volume Two includes photos of the cremation ceremony and other memorial ceremonies.
Both volumes are bilingual, Chinese/English.

****

Venerable Master Hua's Talks on Dharma

Collections of talks given by the Venerable Master on various occasions. Emphasis is placed on how to apply Buddhist principles to personal cultivation. Bilingual, Chinese/English.

The Intention of Patriarch Bodhidharma's Coming from the West.

A Basic Explanation by Venerable Master Hua

A compilation of Venerable Master Hua's lively accounts of the First Buddhist Patriarch in China. Appropriate for both children and adults. Generously illustrated with black and white Chinese brush drawings. Bilingual (Chinese/English). Softcover.

****

The Giant Turtle

Fictional rendering of a Jataka Tale.

English & Bilingual (Chinese/English). Softcover.

Spider Thread

A Basic Explanation by Venerable Master Hua

This is a story of deep significance and results from the encounter of a Bhikshu and a jeweler. In his comment, "Sometimes the smartest people fail to recognize the basic truths about life", the Bhikshu instructs us that every one of us makes our own destiny, in accordance with what we does. The book explains an essential principle in Buddhism —the law of cause and effect — with vivid illustrations and simple words.

Furthermore, it expounds the ineffable strength of repentance and reform. A single generous thought of reform would lend the spider's gossamer enough strength to be a lifeline that saves thousands in the hells. This illustrated story only not nurtures teenagers' good roots, but also offers elders deep inspiration.

Bilingual (Chinese/English) . Softcover.

Proper Dharma Series

A Basic Explanation by Venerable Master Hua

A special edition of a series of Talks on Dharma given by the Venerable Master both in the U.S. and Asia.
Bilingual Chinese/English book and tape.

#2 ~ A Sure Sign of the Proper Dharma

This rousing lecture by the Venerable Master Hua is an avowal of the authenticity of the Shurangama Sutra.

#3 ~ The Great Events of One Hundred Years Are Hazy as if a Dream

Predictions about the future of China made by a monk during the Ming dynasty.

#4 ~ The True Meaning of Taking Refuge

The Venerable Master Hua's explanation of the meaning of becoming a Buddhist disciple.

Audio Cassettes & CD's

Audio Tapes	Language	# of Tapes	Set/Single
Venerable Master Hua's Talks on Dharma (1994)	Bilingual (Mandarin/English)	12	Single
The Sutra in Forty-two Sections Spoken by the Buddha	Bilingual (Mandarin/English)	10	Set
Venerable Master Hua's Talks on Dharma during the 1993 Trip to Taiwan	Bilingual (Mandarin/English)	6	Set
A Sure Sign of the Proper Dharma	Bilingual (Mandarin/English)	2*	Set
The Great Events of One Hundred Years Are Hazy as if a Dream	Bilingual (Mandarin/English)	1*	Set
The True Meaning of Taking Refuge	Bilingual (Mandarin/English)	1*	Set
Guanyin Bodhisattva is Our Brother	English	1	Single
The Patriarch Bodhidharma's Advent in China	English	1	Single
On Investigating Meditation Topic	English	1	Single
The State of Chan Meditation	English	1	Single
Both Good and Evil Exist in a Single Thought	English	1	Single
Cultivate Merit and Virtue without Marks	English	1	Single

Buddhist Gifts
Bookmarks and Post Cards

Buddhist Gifts	Set/Piece
Bookmarks of Venerable Master Hua's Sayings (Scenery)	20 piece
Bookmarks of Venerable Mater Hua's Sayings (Chinese Paintings)	21 piece
Scenery Post Cards of CTTB	38 piece
Picture Set of CTTB (Set)	7 piece

****

Out of the Ground It Emerges:
Wonderful Enlightenment Mountain
by Buddhist Text Translation Society

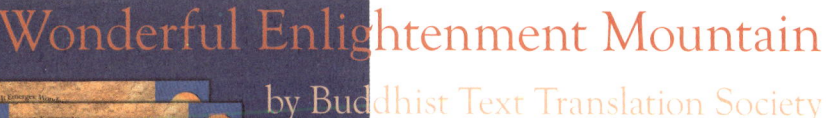

This is special edition celebrating 40 Years of Dharma in the West as transmitted by the Venerable Master Hsuan Hua. It also commemorates the 25th Anniversary of the City of Ten Thousand Buddhas. Bilingual (Chinese/English), Softcover

Dharma Realm Buddhist Association & City of Ten Thousand Buddhas
4951 Bodhi Way, Ukiah, CA 95482 U.S.A.
Tel: (707) 462-0939   Fax: (707) 462-0949

•••

Gold Mountain Monastery
800 Sacramento Street,
San Francisco, CA 94108 U.S.A.
Tel: (415) 421-9112   Fax: (415) 788-6001

The City of the Dharma Realm
1029 West Capitol Avenue,
West Sacramento, CA 95691 U.S.A.
Tel/Fax: (916) 374-8268

The International Translation Institute
1777 Murchison Drive,
Burlingame, CA 94010-4504 U.S.A.
Tel: (650) 692-5912   Fax: (650) 692-5056

Institute for World Religions
(at Berkeley Buddhist Monastery)
2304 McKinley Avenue,
Berkeley, CA 94703 U.S.A.
Tel: (510) 848-3440   Fax: (510) 548-4551

Gold Sage Monastery
11455 Clayton Road,
San Jose, CA 95127 U.S.A.
Tel: (408) 923-7243   Fax: (408) 923-1064

Gold Wheel Monastery
235 North Avenue 58,
Los Angeles, CA 90042 U.S.A.
Tel/Fax: (323) 258-6668

Blessings, Prosperity, and Longevity Monastery
4140 Long Beach Boulevard,
Long Beach, CA 90807 U.S.A.
Tel/Fax: (562) 595-4966

Long Beach Monastery
3361 East Ocean Boulevard,
Long Beach, CA 90803 U.S.A.
Tel/Fax: (562) 438-8902

Avatamsaka Vihara
9601 Seven Locks Road,
Bethesda, MD 20817-9997
Tel/Fax: (301) 469-8300

Gold Summit Monastery
233 First Avenue West,
Seattle, WA 98119 U.S.A.
Tel/Fax: (206) 284-6690

Gold Buddha Monastery
248 E. 11th Avenue, Vancouver,
B.C. V5T 2C3 Canada
Tel/Fax: (604) 709-0248

Avatamsaka Monastery
1009 Fourth Avenue S.W., Calgary,
AB T2P 0K8 Canada
Tel/Fax: (403) 234-0644

Dharma Realm Buddhist Books Distribution Society
11th Floor, 85 Chung Hsiao E. Road,
Sec. 6, Taipei, Taiwan, R.O.C.
Tel: (02) 2786-3022   Fax: (02) 2786-2674

Dharma Realm Sagely Monastery
20, Tung-hsi Shan-chuang,
Hsing-lung Village, Liu-Kuei,
Kaohsiung County, Taiwan, R.O.C.
Tel: (07) 689-3713   Fax: (07) 689-3870

Amitabha Monastery
7, Su-chien-hui,
Chih-nan Village, Shou-Feng,
Hualien County, Taiwan, R.O.C.
Tel: (03) 865-1956   Fax: (03) 865-3426

Prajna Guanyin Sagely Monastery
(formerly Tze Yun Tung)
Batu 5 1/2, Jalan Sungai Besi,
Salak Selatan,
57100 Kuala Lumpur, Malaysia
Tel: (03)7982-6560   Fax:(03) 7980-1272

Deng Bi An Temple
161, Jalan Ampang,
50450 Kuala Lumpur, Malaysia
Tel: (03) 2164-8055   Fax: (03)2163-7118

Lotus Vihara
136, Jalan Sekolah,
45600 Batang Berjuntai,
Selangor Darul Ehsan, Malaysia.
Tel: (03) 3271-9439